M000213375

I'm Not Strange, I Have Autism

I'm Not Strange, I Have Autism
Living with an Autism Spectrum Disorder

Ellen van Gelder

isbn 9789461850645 (paperback)

1st print January 2015

Original title: Ik ben niet vreemd, ik heb autisme

Translations: Avia Dassen, Karin Wouters

Published by Village an imprint of VanDorp Publishers

Postbox 42
3956 ZR  Leersum
The Netherlands

www.vandorp.net / info@vandorp.net

Copyright©2015 Village / VanDorp Publishers The Netherlands
Copyright©2015 Ellen van Gelder

The proceeds of this book are donated by the author to the
autism foundation Stichting Autisme Almere, The Netherlands.

No part of this publication may be reproduced in any form
without the express written permission of the publisher.

ELLEN VAN GELDER

# I'M NOT STRANGE

# STRANGE

LIVING WITH AN AUTISM SPECTRUM DISORDER

# I HAVE

# AUTISM

VILLAGE

*Aren't we all different?*

# Preface

Aren't we all different? What is the being-different in autism? You will notice different things, and notice things differently. It reminds me of a joke a touring guide once told me: 'Ladies and gentlemen, if you look on your left... You will see nothing on your right.'

Is it a curse or a blessing to observe differently and notice different things? In this book, you'll find your answers to those kinds of questions. Many answers will be provided in this collection, but it also becomes clear that things non-autistic people take for granted can be incredibly difficult for people with autism. The book reads like an expedition, and a true explorer cherishes his curiosity, of course.

The non-autistic person has many shared opinions about socialising. There are common ideas on what is considered exciting and what is not; these conceptions give the non-autistic person a sense of connection that they need. People with autism, on the other hand, have much less of a clear insight in social life in general.

I think it would be difficult to have ASD and curiously query the other, but, instead of harvesting answers, you end up estranged from the person without ASD. Why does it annoy people? It appears to be difficult to communicate when one person listens to the guide and looks to the left, while someone else follows their own plan and gazes to the right. What is missing, most of the time, is the curiosity to ask the hows and whys of someone's behaviour. When you have autism, the why-questions are essential in order to finally understand what is meant.

It takes time to clarify, but it is worth more than what we realise at that moment. If I look around me, and see how people normally spend their time, a lack of time can hardly be the problem.

As a community psychiatric caregiver, I met Ellen shortly after she received her ASD-diagnosis in 2010. She had many questions, and my attempts to answer them usually led to more questions. At that time, she didn't realise how difficult she made it for me. In open, honest, and unambiguous reflections she sent me through email, I noticed, in return, how often I didn't realise how difficult I made it for her. Together we learned how to communicate better, and we found new insights. Where talking used to be an incredibly big effort for the both of us, we now have much more space for relaxation. We have become familiar with the other's being different. Ellen's never-ending determination to wanting to understand what someone means, sees, and feels makes her distinctive from others. At present, the majority of the puzzle pieces that constitute her life are within reach; she knows her possibilities and her pitfalls. She handles all of them with a healthy balance of effort and relaxation.

This book gives an insight in the stamina you need to feel at ease in your being different. It is an inspiring book for people with ASD who are looking for balance in their lives, and not just that: this book also gives a beautiful illustration for partners, caregivers, family members, and others who want to know more about autism spectrum disorders, and of the 'being different' that comes with ASD. I wish you, as a reader of this book, a life filled with healthy curiosity, because without it you'll lose an important essence of it. We are all able to connect and meet in this being different, as long as we keep our mutual curiosity.


*Erik Munnik*

Autism expert for 'Focus on Human',
Almere, the Netherlands.

# Index

# INTRODUCTION

It was 22 January 2010, the year in which I turned 40, when I heard that I have Asperger's Syndrome: ASD, a disorder within the autism spectrum*. On the one hand, despite being prepared for this diagnosis, it still brought up the necessary emotions. On the other hand, it was a relief: the last piece of the puzzle finally fell into place. In the meanwhile, I had been diagnosed with several other disorders, amongst which Tourette syndrome, obsessive compulsive disorders, and emetophobia**. Apparently, my autism never surfaced really openly; it was a clear example of so-called 'hidden autism'.

I suspect that, just like me, there are many other adults who were diagnosed at a later age. This is probably due to the fact that there is a lot more knowledge on autism these days, and hidden autism is still widespread, especially amongst women. With this book, which is partly autobiographical, I'd like to give the reader an insight in the world of someone with autism. I would like to do this in an accessible way and chose to do it in an A-through-Z structure. Frequently I will quote some brothers and sisters-in-autism, as I like to call them, because they will often experience things differently than I do. Not every autist is like the other, you know? ;-) The quotes in this book are taken from fellow members of a forum for people with ASD.

Over the years it's become clear to me that autism has to do with processing information in a different way. This book will also discuss some scientific backgrounds (which can be found in the 'Theories' section), but I would mainly like to keep it practical. I hope that people with a disorder in the autistic spectrum (henceforth, ASD) can recognise themselves, but the same goes for people who are still in search of answers. This book also is an appropriate read for people who live with someone with ASD, and would like to get to know more about the topic.

Ellen van Gelder

*Autism Spectrum Disorder in DSM-5:*
*This entails that there will no longer be new diagnoses of Classic Autism, PDD-NOS, and Asperger Syndrome.*

*Under much attention from the media, DSM-5, the most recent handbook for psychiatry, was launched on 17 May 2014. This is the manual for psychiatrists, which includes all diagnoses that are filed under psychiatry and which criteria they adhere to. In this brand-new version, much has changed for autism as a diagnosis. The current diagnoses PDD-NOS, Asperger Syndrome, and Classic Autism are put together under one name: Autism Spectrum Disorder (ASD). The term 'spectrum' here denotes that there is a diversity in the ways in which autism can out itself. In the DSM-5, there is a possibility to specify if the ASD is either mild or severe.*

*Source: NVA (Nederlandse Vereniging voor Autisme, the Dutch Association for Autism)*

*** Emetophobia: intense fear for vomiting or seeing other people vomit.*

# ASPERGER'S

The day after I received my diagnosis – when it was still called Asperger's instead of ASD – I wrote the following:

*Maybe needless to say, but no, this isn't a story about a delicious asparagus soup bubbling away on my stove at the moment. To bring on the hard facts: since Friday I know that I have Asperger's, a disorder in the autistic spectrum... No, I'm not surprised... now I finally know why I always act so 'weird'... When I was younger, I was spit out and excluded, but every time I tried to be part of the group again. When children were playing hide and seek, I would stand near them and announce, 'I'm also joining you', and then I would hide. I didn't realise at all that they didn't like me.*

*I've always tried to be part of a group. In secondary school I was bullied and teased continuously (they would imitate my tics; I also have Gilles de la Tourette). Later I found out that they bullied me because of my behaviour, and that my tics were a great way to do it. Strangely enough, I would still invite the bullies for my birthday every single year.*

*During English class in third form, we were allowed to bring a cassette (you know, those rectangular things with a tape inside that you put in a cassette deck) with music to listen to through headphones. When it was my turn, I crammed my cassette tape full with one track, my favourite Gazebo song: "I Like Chopin" and put it on in class. When the song started for the second time, there were some indignant responses from the classroom, and when the song – which I thought was amazing – started for the third time, people started to get really annoyed. I truly didn't understand what I had done wrong. It was a good song, wasn't it?*

*I also did teacher training and worked in education for some time. My preference for being around children might be explained by the fact that children are very honest. I remember a comment from a girl who told me, 'Miss, when I look at you, you always look away'. I started to pay attention to this. I have hardly had to deal with my other nonverbal expressions. My facial expression remains neutral (with the exception of my tics), and I hardly gesture when I speak.*

*At one point I was ready to be admitted to the psychiatric wing of the hospital. My colleagues and I were having a final drink at the school where I worked at the time. I said, 'Cheers, to my madness!' Nobody laughed! How strange?! I was very surprised at their lack of response, and, in all honesty, a teensy bit disappointed.*

*Conflicts and miscommunications, these happen to me all the time. At one point I figured out that, apparently, it is normal to have to interpret things. That's very difficult when you take everything literally. What does 'See you soon!' or 'I'll phone you soon!' mean? Or 'You'll hear from me,' that expression doesn't make any sense at all! It really drives me mad sometimes! But when I start asking questions, I'm the one who drives people insane. I simply don't understand it sometimes. I have often felt and still feel so powerless, because I don't understand the world around me. I could write a book about it. You know what? Maybe I will.*

*I'm going to do groceries in a bit. Edit: I'm going to do groceries now.*

I retrieved those past memories with my best friend, one of the few who has always accepted me the way that I am. She's one of the few people on this planet who has incredible empathic skills. Even people without ASD can take her as an example!

# BIG PICTURE

This chapter isn't about big pictures, but about missing them. Although I do sometimes wonder what the deal is with blowing up pictures... I tend to lose the big picture quite quickly. I notice it in my own house, where it's usually a mess. I don't want it to be that way, though, and I always swear to improve it. For some reason, however, I am incapable of having a clean and orderly house. It's difficult enough to start doing the dishes, because it's arranged so uncoordinatedly on the counter. The only thing that's really ordered well is my CD-collection; it's perfectly organised in alphabetical order in storage boxes.

My garden is pretty big, and I tend to lose some structure there as well. Last year, I divided my garden in four sections, and I clear out one section at a time. When I don't, I'm likely to start clearing things randomly, and will lose track of where I'm at.

When someone asks me multiple things at the time, I tend to lose the bigger picture as well. I'll think about the first thing they asked, and I'll remember only part of the second question, and then there's a problem. What should I do now? What is the most important? Those are questions I ask myself. Eventually I freeze, because I lost the main point.

Karen:
*'When I lose the big picture? When it comes to complex tasks, where I have to do more things simultaneously. When our house is messy. My surroundings have to be organised, or else I won't be able to function.*

*I have to do chores one step at a time, so I have to divide them up in steps first. For example: clearing the room so I can cook. First, taking all the cups, glasses, plates, etc. that are in the room, and sorting them on the counter. Then, putting the papers in the room in a logical spot, or stacking them. Then, hanging all the coats on the coat rack... etc. And only then I'd be ready to start cooking.'*

Sandra:

*'Having a clear picture clears my head a bit. It's always busy in my head, so it's difficult to keep things in order up there. Having predictability, clear structures, and clear chores and orders help me to retain that overview, enabling me to do what I have to do.*

*It's not like a ritual, I really don't care about those, but it works as a foundation or support. They are a type of guidelines, if you will. It is exhausting if I have to keep figuring out what and how to do something; I can't really do that automatically. Those famous autism-puzzle pieces have to be thought together, as it were. The more unrest in my head or around me, the more difficult it becomes. Time and social pressure (like, 'Come on, you have to understand that,' or 'No, don't go on auto-pilot') are the most devastating things in that respect. It often wears me out so much that I'll literally see stars of being fatigued.*

*In stressful situations I'll have too much on my mind, and I lose the big picture as well. Following conversations in a room where multiple conversations are happening tire me as well. The same goes for overseeing traffic situations. When it's calm and neat around me, I feel less like my head's going to explode.'*

# CHANGES

I find it very difficult when things go differently than planned. It used to be much harder than it is now, though; now I take into account that someone might just cancel an appointment, or that someone might show up later, or not show up at all. Realising this makes my life a little bit easier.

Changes in relation to modern technology are my biggest stumbling-blocks. Take a new website layout, for instance. It may cost days or weeks for me to get used to them. Last year, I bought a pretty modern phone, and lo and behold, I've gotten used to it. I also have a ridiculously large TV, LED or HD, I have no idea, but it's pretty cool! Secretly I get nostalgic and want to go back to the era in which modern devices didn't play such a big role. Of course, I see the usefulness of all of those gadgets, but it doesn't balance out the stress that comes with it. You always have to be available, and when they stop working, who fixes them for you? Also, they're ridiculously expensive.

Changing to a different social worker is the hardest. It takes months or longer before I start to get used to them. For my housekeeping duties, I have a good help now, and she understands how she has to deal with me. I won't change to a new help any time soon, because it takes up too much energy and it's not relevant for now.

Khadijah:
*There are things I want to change continuously, and things I don't want to change at all. There are things that change without me wanting to, and realising this change takes some time. Think*

*of, for instance, a new taste sensation. Only when I evaluate the taste, I change the way I cook, so that everything around this new sensation changes in my system. It's pretty rigorous. I also have combinations of changing and not changing. For instance, I like to keep my furniture and knick-knacks, but I do like to rearrange them all the time. I moved house recently, and I tried to keep as much of them as I could, though I had to add some things to it. Nevertheless, it felt very good to do it like this. Something that never changes is my favourite colour (purple). Of course, I wear different colours and I have stuff that isn't purple, but I have to have something purple at all times. It doesn't even have to be visible immediately. There have been times where I haven't put purple in my clothing, but I'd have a purple hair accessory. I'll find some purple item I take with me. The changes I find most difficult are the ones where I have to bend over backwards to do things that I decide to do differently. It is easier when someone asks me to do something differently. For instance, I'm wearing coat A, because I always wear this coat when I go see my sons. Suddenly I think that coat B might look better with my outfit, colour-wise. I'll take coat B out of the closet to wear when I leave, but when I wear it, it just doesn't feel right. Then I'll change back to coat A. I've come far enough to wear coat B instead of coat A, and no longer doubt this change. It's the same when I have to change from winter coat to summer coat, and vice versa. These are only a couple of examples, but I could fill an entire book with them.'*

Anne:

*'I respond similar to most changes: when I'm feeling well, I can cope pretty well with them. If I'm not feeling that well, a relatively little change can completely shut me down.'*

Rob B:
*'I know by now that change is just part of life. I'm geared to cope when things go differently in practice, but sometimes I can feel uncertain and bothered by it. By knowing this I don't grow angry or respond negatively in another way, which takes up no energy at all. However, having to realise that I know takes an awful lot of energy.'*

Karen:
*'I can deal with change, but it has to be announced. I have to know in advance what I'm dealing with.'*

Sandra:
*'I can handle change pretty well; it's a fact of life that things deviate from their plan every day. I don't need everything to be the same. I can start to feel really anxious when I'm in an environment in which I have to do something according to strict rules. For that reason, I left the day centre, whose activities were focused on autism specifically. For some it would be paradise, but not for me, though. Changes can cause some tension.*

*I can deal with change in terms of a change in a known environment, but it does take a while for me to get used to them. It doesn't feel familiar anymore, which also means that the picture that I have of the place will have to change. That usually takes some time. At the day centre, they took away the cupboards; now, the space looks completely different. I'm not going to complain, but I miss the old layout. I have to say that the old layout wasn't exactly practical for most people, and it is important for the social workers to be able to have a good idea of the space and the people.*

*Moving house is also a good example. After my last move it took me a year to update the pictures I had of 'home'. It took the same amount of time before really experiencing my new house as my home. Only now, the biking trails are 'my routes'. This feels now so familiar, that I don't want to leave this place anymore!*

*Change in my everyday structure can mean that I am completely distraught, because my guidelines aren't relevant anymore. It drains me, because I have to consciously think of what I meant to do that day.'*

# COMMUNICATION

I always fail in this area. I really don't understand why people communicate so vaguely.

Saying 'A' when they mean 'B'... A good example is the following, which happened at my previous reintegration office. My coach was going to look up some things for me, and phone me about it on Thursday. When someone tells me that they'll phone me, I assume that they will do it, right? That Thursday I waited for that phone call, to no avail. By six o'clock I was pretty pissed off and thought, 'forget it.' Promises, promises... In moments like these, I feel slightly murderous intentions arising in myself. Later, during the next appointment, my coach told me, 'I didn't have news yet, which is why I didn't phone you.'

My jaw dropped! I can't know that there isn't any news, can I? And didn't we agree that she would phone me? I'll contain myself at such a moment, even though my blood is boiling. I will tell them, calm and composed, that I would prefer it if they would give me a call anyway, because that was our agreement and I tend to grow agitated as a result. The coach told me that she would keep it into account, but the next time she did the exact same thing. I almost reached my level of explosion, and we had a little bit of a row in which I shared my opinion quite bluntly.

At those moments I find myself wondering, 'When someone tells me to call, should I take into account that it might not happen?' Because they tell you 'A': I will call you. But maybe she means 'B': maybe I will not? Something like that? It seems quite simple, to just not have any expectations. Unfortunately it doesn't work that way for me, because I'd like to be prepared when someone might call. When I'm prepared, I will have my phone on hand and mentally ready myself to receive a phone call. These things cause quite some restlessness for me, because I shouldn't expect something, or maybe I should...?

This Internet era hasn't always made the life of a person with ASD easier. I've had many misunderstandings, through email for example. This escalated to the point where it ruined friendships and relationships. For this reason I decided that I will no longer have arguments and/or misunderstandings out through email. Preferably I'd do it in face-to-face conversation, and if that can't be realised, then at least over the telephone.

Something I don't understand at all when emailing is the salutation and closing. You can start an email in so many different ways... Think about hi, hello, dear, good day, dearest... Although the salutation isn't that difficult, the closing is what usually causes trouble. You can use yours sincerely, yours truly, yours faithfully, kind regards, best wishes, cheers, love, x, xx, xxx, xxxx etc... and I've probably not mentioned half of the possibilities.

I understand that you can't end a formal letter with a series of crosses, and if I write my best friend I won't sign off using 'yours faithfully'. But oh, there are so many possibilities between those two, it could drive someone insane! I can get so confused that it makes me feel completely powerless.

However, there are still many misunderstandings in 'live' contact. Among affecting other elements of perception, autism is a disorder that affects the processing of information. In 'live communication' I always distinguish three ways of communicating that often happen at the same time: verbal (the words), non-verbal (the facial expressions), and gesturing. As people with ASD can't detect all three of these channels of communication at once, they will often miss parts of the entire message. For example, when a friend is annoyed over something and she tells me about it, I should be able to see from her face that she is annoyed. But, when she tells me this in a friendly voice, I often don't notice that she is annoyed and the message doesn't come across. If I would have been able to detect all signals, I would have read her face, seen her body language, and as such understood the entire message.

Understanding body language is something that I've learnt to do by reading up on it and subsequently observing it in people. I can often read facial expressions, as long as they are clear. Anger and sadness are the easiest, but the grey area of other emotions are still difficult. This is something that many autists have trouble with: the separate ways of communication, let alone the combination of two or three of these channels.

Rob (after a meeting with fellow autists):
*'I notice that I'll often look for the socially acceptable behaviour at such moments. I have an extensive collection of card-indices*

*in my head, to use a metaphor. In these indices, there are many different types of people and social situations, which I have provided with additional notes from the past and copies of the ways other people behave. When I talk to someone, I pull the right card out of the index, as it were. Does someone need consolation? For women, heartache: 'Console, put an arm around her, ask if she's doing okay, how she feels, listen to her, etc.' Man, heartache: '(curse) man, what the f\*ck? Want a beer?' Something like that. At this stage I wonder if I'm not a cold analyst, since I'm reasoning like this in the NT-world\*. But... it works. For people with autism things work in a completely different way. Yesterday, amongst autists, I tried to break a silence in the way I'd do it with my NT-friends, since it's socially desirable to not drop silences. Later, I realised, 'These are fellow autists. They probably think silences are fine, because they constantly think of other things, just like I do.' Another eye-opener.'*

Kimberley:
*'Especially oral communication is difficult for me. Communicating is easier in writing, but even that takes some effort. In written communication I especially experience difficulties in structuring what I write.*

*Oral communication is always laborious. In the moment I often don't know how to respond to someone; I usually realise how I should have done it later on. That's pretty tiresome, especially when it happens in important conversations. I am easily taken aback by a question, and end up being unable to talk any more. My head freezes, so to speak. Sometimes I notice that I take things differently than the way they were intended. I will then respond, but only later realise that the answer wasn't*

*appropriate for what the person meant. I think it's a shame that*
*there are so few people who will say, 'I didn't mean that', and so*
*many people who just drop it. I don't have examples right now,*
*though. Maybe I'll think of something later, but usually these*
*instances are just too painful for me, and I would rather not*
*share them.'*

Hans:
*'I often don't know what to say in real-life situations. I am much*
*better at communication through email etc. I also notice that*
*I can enjoy serene silences during conversations in certain*
*circumstances (these serene silences feel differently than the*
*awkward ones, which also depends on the company).'*

Anna:
*'Lately I have more contact with people whilst walking my dog.*
*Yesterday I even chatted a little with a girl who apparently*
*doted on dogs (admittedly, even a conversation with a child can*
*frighten me). It's stupid to be so nervous when unknown people*
*start talking to you.*

*It's been two months since the end of my social skills training*
*(SST). I've probably learnt something from it, but I don't yet put*
*a lot of it in practice. Talking to strangers and other strange*
*people still isn't a hobby of mine.'*

*\*NT stands for neurotypical, the normal world.*
*See the chapter 'Neurotypical' for more information.*

# COMORBIDITY

There are many people who have another diagnosis, in addition to their ASD. This phenomenon is called comorbidity: having two or more chronic disorders at the same time. Amongst others, disorders that often occur with ASD are:

- ADD/ADHD: Attention Deficit Hyperactivity Disorder
- OCD: Obsessive Compulsive Disorder
- Gilles de la Tourette syndrome
- Depression
- Anxiety disorders
- Addiction
- Eating disorders
- Psychosis
- Behavioural disorders
- Mood disorders

The difficult thing with comorbidity is that it can mask ASD. It can also be the other way around: ASD might mask another disorder as well. As a consequence, ASD might not always be discovered, or discovered in time or another disorder might stay hidden.

As I'm writing this, I'm thinking about Tourette syndrome. I've been suffering from Tourette syndrome since I was seven years old – I was officially diagnosed when I was 29. This masked my ASD, because there are many similarities and overlaps between the two, and the characteristics that are part of both Tourette and ASD were said to be caused by my Tourette.

Sometimes a disorder can develop as a result of ASD; this is often the case with depression. People with ASD can be under so much stress, adversity, and incomprehension that a depression is almost inevitable. I personally was 'granted' some depressions as well. I've learned from it, though: by setting boundaries in my life I'm able to prevent a next depression. For instance, I no longer go to birthdays, simply because it takes too much energy. I work part-time and divide appointments throughout the week, instead of all on one day – something I used to do.

Hans:
*'I'm not comorbid; sometimes I'm just morbid.'*

Kimberley:
*'Officially, I don't have comorbid disorders. But that doesn't mean that they're not actually there. In my family, ADHD and dyslexia occur a lot. I was tested for dyslexia, and the test said I didn't have it. But I thought the way it was tested was weird, and the lady who tested me made me feel a bit uncomfortable, so I'm not sure if I have actually don't have it. Through my studies, I know a thing or two about dyslexia. For instance, automatic processes in the brain are difficult for dyslectics: it simply takes longer for dyslectics to know how to write a certain word. That's why it becomes more and more difficult to diagnose it at later age. I know I make less errors in my writing now, because I've learnt how to write them. However, when I reread some of the writing assignments from my first year in secondary school... Those were riddled with mistakes. And that was after having them checked by the spell checker.*

*I don't think I 'fully' have ADD or ADHD, but I do know it affects me a little. I notice that I have difficulties focusing, especially when I'm studying. I'm also a terribly associative thinker – I can easily associate with any and every word – and I keep losing track of the material I was studying. I'm not that good at sitting still either, because I feel like I have to do this, and then do that, before actually sitting down and doing what I'm supposed to be doing. I take after my mother (who has ADHD), and it really annoys me. Because all those little instances of 'I quickly need to do this' take up a lot of time when added up.'*

Natasja:
*'The combination of autism and migraine is incredibly difficult. Because of my autism, I tend to get over-stimulated and stressed out, which gives me migraines.'*

# DETAILS

Being someone with ASD, I'm one for details. Sadly, this often leads to annoyance in people around me.

My observation of details becomes most visible when you're talking to me. When someone tells me something, I will trail off, thinking about the details. This leads me to take the story completely out of context, and I no longer know what the person wanted to tell me in the first place. The worst-case scenario is when the person I'm talking to no longer remembers what they wanted to say.

When I listen to a story, it comes to me in parts rather than as a whole, literally word for word. A story of 333 words, for instance, doesn't come to me as a story, but as 333 separate units. These units have to be merged together into sentences in my head, and only then into a story. When I don't understand one unit, I feel like I have to clarify what exactly that unit means, because otherwise I won't understand the story. In one way or another, my brain is programmed to absorb each piece, each detail, of a story. For me, a story is complete only when all of the pieces make sense. So, let's say someone tells me something that consists out of nine 'pieces' of a puzzle. If the top right piece is missing for me, then the essence of the story is lost for my understanding, because the story isn't complete.

The difficult thing is that, if I keep interrupting someone to ask them for clarification about a certain part of their story, they aren't able to finish their story properly. This used to happen a lot, and I started to annoy people in doing so. I'd ask them to explain every single detail of the story. This also made me a difficult student in secondary school, because I would demand a lot of attention by asking so many questions. That is just one example of the 'different' ways in which I process information.

I've been trying to reprogram my brain for some time now. When I'm in a conversation with someone, I force myself to let the other finish completely. If I don't understand a detail of their story, I tell myself to let it go. It definitely takes a lot of effort, but I am able to do it! And I'm proud of myself for doing so. Of course, it doesn't always quite pan out, but I try to interrupt them friendlier than I used to. I'd say something like, 'Would you mind if I interrupt you for a moment? Otherwise I won't understand the story.'

In short, I adapt. I'm convinced this leads to a happier life for me. The slogan 'they'll have to take me the way I am' sounds nice, but it doesn't work like that in practice. As long as I feel that I remain true to myself and feel better by adapting my behaviour slightly, I don't have any problems with it.

It must be said, though, that the way in which this focus on details surfaces differs from person to person. For an autistic friend of mine, for instance, it's much more visual. When he's been into a room he had never been in before, he'll still remember every little thing he saw in that room afterwards. When it comes to details, I'm more focused on sounds.

A while back, I was in the theatre to see a show of a comedian. At a certain moment, my friend said, "I'm so distracted by the fact that one button on his shirt has a different colour than the others". When I looked closely, I saw that he did indeed have one different button. He was wearing a shirt with five buttons, four of which were black, but one was red. I hadn't even noticed. Another example is that I showed him a video of a couple of friends on my phone, when he told me. 'Gee, they have a nice coffee-maker!' It was a small detail in the background of the video. Being either focused on auditory or visual details can be incredibly exhausting.

Because of my fellow autists, I started to pay attention to details even more. I can use the visual details for my photography (one of my big passions). I really would like to stress that noticing details can work positively as well. I can be found by a river or canal bank pretty often. I'll be on the lookout to take photographs of insects, using my macro lens. I find it incredibly fascinating to see these little creatures on my computer screen. Things you can barely see with the naked eye are suddenly enlarged. That's something I can really revel in, something I really enjoy.

Sandra:

'I can really get stuck on details, thinking about them a lot. When I want to continue talking about these details, the conversation has already taken a different direction pretty much every time. I try to refrain from going back to the things that have been talked about already, but I do have to think about that and control myself. Sometimes I think it's really sad that I've become so aware of this, because it makes me less spontaneous.'

Natasja:

'I find that I notice things that many other people miss. When walking through the woods, for instance, I see the smallest creatures and plants. I do like it, but sometimes it's very exhausting to see so much. When it comes to sounds, I always hear everything as well, while others only hear it when I point it out to them. When cleaning, I have learnt to be a little less nitpicky. If I have to wait until I have the energy to actually *clean everything properly, I'll never do it. Plus, it's difficult enough for me to keep things tidy as they are.'*

Hans:

*'I also notice details really often. I like them especially when it comes to music, and I think I have the same for nature. Although, I don't really like going outside, so I'm not confronted with the 'Great Outdoors' all too much. When someone says something funny without intending it (which might not even be related to the contents of what they're saying), due to their phrasing, for instance, I can crack up a little. But it must be noted that, when phrasing is unclear, I get caught in trying to figure out the meaning. Details can be fun, but when I have to make sense of chaos – cleaning my house, for example – getting so caught up in details can also work as a burden.'*

Kimberley:

*'I tend to notice many details, and sometimes that's cool. We have many birds in our neighbourhood, and I can really enjoy just lying in bed in the morning, with my eyes closed, listening to the birdsong. I also like seeing birds searching for little twigs in the garden, or seeing little lambs jumping around in the grass when I'm on the bus. I hear a lot in music as well. It's very handy when I'm playing, because I don't need to count. I know I have to play when I hear a certain instrument do a certain thing. That is, however, also the drawback: if that person isn't there, I can no longer play accurately.*

*Noticing these details can be incredibly exhausting. The university I go to has free Wi-Fi, which it says on these blue, flickering lights in one of our lecture halls. It kept distracting me, because I saw every single flash. I'm really happy they changed them to green lights that are on continuously.*

*Sometimes I can lose the overall picture because I'm so focused on details. When I don't understand something in my study material, I'll look it up in a book or through Google. It happens on occasion that it's still not entirely clear to me, and I'll keep searching, even though it isn't always that important.'*

# EMPATHY

To cut straight to the point: I am capable of feeling empathy, and maybe ten times as much as people who don't have ASD. I'll illustrate it, of course. I can imagine that the attentive reader won't just agree with this bold statement.

First off: empathy works differently for me. The difficult thing for me is that I often am unable to actually feel what people feel, which means that I don't feel when I 'should' be empathetic. Whether or not anyone should feel empathetic is a different discussion entirely.

Usually I respond using reasoning, and I appear very socially capable when doing so. Since I am so aware of the fact that these things occur through a detour with me, I'm alert and listen well to the other person. Of course, it doesn't always quite work out, but you don't have to have ASD to fail at this sometimes. Something still engraved in my memory is when I accused a friend of having promised to give me a massage, but him never actually doing it. I was so busy with myself and my being disgruntled that I lost my empathic capacity for a moment; I chose to talk to him about it when he and his family were going through a tough time, which needed his attention. I've felt incredibly guilty and sad over this.

In general, I can say that I'm a person who tries hard to put myself in the person's shoes, to understand them. When I am unable to do this, I mention this situation to my therapist or coach who comes to my house. I keep doing this, because I am aware of my limitations in communication. I notice that I'm very cautious most of the time, because I want to do the best I can to not hurt people. It does pay off, because my communication skills improve, but it also takes a lot of energy: it's not easy to find the balance. Sometimes I'm exhausted from trying to figure things out in situations where communication and empathy are important.

When it comes to feeling with someone... Of course I can sympathise with people; stories about children can be very touching, for instance. I find myself crying on the phone when one of my friends' children isn't well. Empathy comes easy when it's about kids, but I'm able to find it for adults as well.

Kimberley:

'Yes, I have empathy. I am able to genuinely feel with someone; what's on the news can really get to me, for instance. What I'm bad at, though, is showing empathy. I've learnt to feel with someone when they're enthusiastic, which I used to be unable to do. I can recall a situation when someone was really happy about something, and I responded by asking, 'Why are you telling me this?' I couldn't really do anything with it back then. Now I can say something like, 'How nice!' and ask questions about what happened to them. When someone is sad or bursts into tears, however, I still find it really difficult to respond; I'll freeze and don't know what to do. I do sympathise with them on the inside, but I have no idea what to say or what to do to make things better. That's something I have trouble with, especially when it's a friend. It feels like failing, and it makes me feel very uncomfortable.'

Natasja:

'People without autism have more of a "what you see is what you get" attitude. When it's not clear from your face or noticeable from your actions that you sympathise with them, you're not *doing it. And that's where all the descriptions of symptoms of autism come from: people with autism behave differently, so autism is a social disorder. It's apparently very difficult to look for underlying causes.'*

Karen:

*'I do have empathy, but I find it hard to console someone. When someone's crying I don't really touch him or her. I do talk to them and ask what's going on, and sometimes I'll give the other person a glass of water if they want one.'*

Sandra:

*'I feel many things, but I can't always respond to them quickly and adequately. Responsiveness is something people measure your empathy with and this is where I fall short. Since I feel so much, I tend to seclude myself, because it can arouse a lot of emotion in me as well. Growing up I learnt to make the difference between what I get from others and what I feel for myself; but obviously this depends on how I feel at a given moment. My friends haven't told me that they think I don't feel enough, but I know that I am more analytic in my responses than other people are. And that's something that gives other people space to talk to me. I console people by hugging, especially children, and I like doing that: words are often just words. However, not everyone and every situation lends itself for it, and just like many neurotypicals I don't always know what to say.'*

Anne:

*'It appears that people without ASD can feel how another person feels. I can analyse how someone feels, but there is no real empathy there.'*

Hans:

*'I think I'm pretty empathetic, but it does help when someone tells me what exactly their problem is. I don't really like situations where someone suddenly starts telling me their life story. When it's someone I know, I can genuinely feel with them, especially when I've been through something similar. I try to imagine how their misery feels, and I'll often feel it physically. That feeling may not be as strong as when I would've gone through the exact same situation myself, but I'm not insensitive. However, there's a lot that I find hard to imagine, because some things can be unimaginable. I'll try to reason through why something is unethical or unjust or something similar. When the government dupes someone I think it's unjust, but in all honesty I think the state itself is unjust and wrongful (although there might have been elections, I think that politicians who are guilty of deceiving voters should just leave the political stage).'*

# E XHAUSTION

I feel exhausted really often. This is especially due to the amount of stimuli I have to process during any given day. I will become fatigued if I don't dose it well enough. I have to stick to my boundaries constantly. When there are people, there has to be communication, and that causes over-stimulation, tiredness, and in the end exhaustion (see the chapter 'Stimuli' for more information on this). If I don't mind my boundaries, I need an entire week to refuel. The problem here is that it can't always be foreseen. Sometimes things just happen out of my control; one of my pets might need to go to the vet, for instance. When this causes too many activities on one day, I get fatigued very quickly.

Sometimes, though, things are simply too much fun not to do them. I don't always feel like taking into consideration, 'Doesn't this activity make me too tired?' I try to get the best out of my life, and I accept that sometimes exhaustion is just a consequence of good things.


Kimberley:
*'I feel exhausted on a regular basis. Everything takes so much energy. When I have a lot to do, I already feel tired just thinking about it. On top of that, I'll sleep badly because my head is just clouded with stress. And when I don't feel well, I'm also fatigued quickly. There are periods where I'll sleep ridiculous amounts. One in every so often there is no particular reason for it; I can go to bed at half past seven, and sleep till nine in the morning.'*

Sandra:
*'I feel tired every single day. That's why I go to bed in the middle of the day for one and a half to two hours. I'll make it pretty dark (not completely dark, because it's day). Preferably I'd have my cat with me, daydreaming a little, sleeping some, and just letting everything go.*

*If I step over my boundaries, I'll feel ill and fall ill. I notice the same thing in my daughter; we can both get a fever that'll pass in a couple of hours (that is, if we take our rest). My head and muscles start aching, especially my legs, I get problems with balance (I become dizzy and nauseated; the doctor says I have something Meniere-like), I will start seeing auras as* with migraine, I become curt in my responses, and I don't quite register what people tell me.'

Hans:

'Normally I'm alone a lot (I live on my own and rarely go out), and after a couple of days of going to the day centre I have to cath up on my sleep and take a nap for a while (usually two to three hours). After social situations outside (travelling with public transportation, crowdedness, autism-meeting), I need those extra naps for a couple of days in a row. Still then during ongoing social or other interactions I can lose track of my story in the middle of a sentence, a couple of times in a row, plus the necessary moments of staring, of course.'

AQ:

'When it comes to being exhausted, I can be very short: I only am tired when I am in physical pain or when I'm busy in my head. Since this happens almost every day, I'm used to stepping over my boundaries and I don't even notice anymore. Why, you ask? Well, having both disturbances of equilibrium and ADHD isn't the best combination.

I'm never really fatigued due to over-stimulation. It's more the opposite; I'll get bored when I'm not challenged.'

# FREEDOM

When I turned eighteen, I wanted to live on my own as soon as I could, independently and free. I went to study in a town in the east of the country to do teacher training, because I wanted to become a teacher. My first room was a little attic room, three by two metres, with two little windows. There was a cattle market close by, and they would sell every Monday. There were cows, and they were all mooing as if their life depended on it. I do miss the noise sometimes. So, I've been living independently in relative freedom since I am eighteen; first I lived in a room, and eventually I ended up in a different town, in the middle of the country. I have a rental house with a garden, and I'm really happy with it.

Since I receive my PIP (Personal Independance Payment), I've had help with my living situation. I think I have had help for about six years now. I receive a budget per year, and I use it to hire people to help me with my administration, arranging things (such as calling organisations), making a schedule, doing the groceries, and offering an attentive ear. In addition, I have a maid over every week to help me with my housekeeping.

Before I received the PIP, I was even more careful than I am now. I think I'd be fair in saying that the help that I currently receive prevents me from being admitted to the hospital again. Without this aid I would lose track of everything. My head would explode as a result of stress. I would get depressed again, and end up in that same vicious circle that I've been in way too often. I have been admitted a couple of times and I've been through day treatment, because I couldn't make it on my own. Needless to say, I'm incredibly happy with all this help!

Hans:

*I'm pretty free living on my own, and have lived on my own for fifteen years already! Before that, I lived with my parents. During the first eleven years of living on my own, I also had a full-time job. This left me incapable of doing housework when I got home, because I was so tired. I cooked once a week for the entire week, and ate the same thing every day. I had a repertoire of three similar wok meals: nasi goreng, bami goreng, and macaroni, and I didn't really vary from that. On occasion I would opt for a microwaved meal, a snack, or a take-away meal. My house became more and more messy, and I would leave my dishes in the sink for months. Before cooking, I would sometimes rinse the things that I needed, but sometimes I wouldn't even do that. I knew it wasn't really good to live that way, but I didn't know where to start clearing up or cleaning, even if I had the energy.*

*For me, my diagnosis was a way that opened a lot of doors for me; it opened the door to care and coaching in particular. I've had a coach for four years now, and as I don't have a job, I have time and energy for housekeeping as well. In the beginning, I had a housekeeping help come over twice a week. We'd clear out and clean the house in steps. Now it's just keeping up with it every week. Slowly but surely, I'm getting better at that. When I experience a drawback, I might slip back and won't be able to do my housekeeping for a while. Luckily I'll be able to pick it up quite quickly again. A couple of weeks without housekeeping help (when they're on holiday, for example) isn't that big of a problem anymore.*

*For now, or maybe for good, I still need help. And that's what makes the difference between being able to live independently and being evicted from my house.'*

Kimberley:

*'I don't live on my own, but with my dad. I expect to live independent with some help in the future. I will have to keep my house orderly, arrange my finances for myself, and keep myself fed properly. I expect to be needing help when it comes to arranging things, because I also have telephone phobia. I think my mother will be able to help me with that for a while – she'll make the necessary phone calls for me – but that isn't a long-term solution, of course. So... I'll have to find a way to get over that fear, or find help for those kinds of things.'*

Natasja:

*'Having lived in an institution for a couple of years, I am happy to live independently again. Although I did have my own house, living in that institution has done me more wrong than right. You could say that it made me stronger and more independent, especially due to their neglect, but the price to pay was much too high. I now have help from someone who also has autism, and who has an autistic son – an adult who lives independently. I pay for his help with money from my PIP. I am in charge of how and when, and for that reason I consider it a sign of strength: I do what I can do, and where I need help I can decide who I will ask to do that for me.'*

Sandra:

*'I live independently, with a cat, bunny, and two kids. I don't have any help for in and around the house. I have enough insight*

in my own life, including finances, and because I don't have a job, I have enough energy for housekeeping duties. In times of sickness, it was obvious that this was difficult for me, but I didn't have any help then, either. At most there were people to help me structuring my days, but in general I can do that on my own. I'll run into trouble when I just need an extra pair of hands to do something together, because I'm simply too tired to do it on my own. So that was that, and those coaching conversations take up more energy than they would help me with. That was before my diagnosis. It's all good until extra things are added to the way things generally go, such as my impending kitchen renovation. These things turn my life upside down, but I'll go through them on my own all the same. I have no idea what a coach would be able to do in those situations, because it has to happen, and nothing can be done about that. I'm the one who plans and arranges everything.

I do have home support for my son. She takes care of both my children, so I am able to go out to dance, after having spent eleven years at home without a babysitter. I can forget about being a mother for a while and enjoy what I do. My son is autistic; my daughter doesn't have that diagnosis, but she does have ADD and a gigantic fear of abandonment. That wasn't something you could dump on your average babysitter, so I arranged a trustworthy, young lady with a specialty in orthopedagogy. The children have learned a lot from that; mum leaves, and she also returns. After two years, they've come as far as being able to go to sleep when I'm not home yet; that is, most of the time. It's an incredible victory I'd never have expected. I already thought it quite an accomplishment that they stayed in bed while I was gone.

45

*This support lady also accompanies my son to scary appointments, because he can get really anxious. For instance, she'll join us when there are needles and pain involved for an appointment in hospital. I can really feel the support, because she thinks and helps along, which makes me feel like I'm not alone in all of it.'*

Anna:

*'I no longer have my indication for counselling, but you don't see me crying about it. I also applied for going to the day centre, which also was denied. They then immediately withdrew the indication I already had. Their main motivation: I am already under treatment elsewhere, can arrange help via insurance, and above all I have a partner who can run our household.*

*I understand that there have to be cutbacks and that the "welfare state" is practically dead, but it still isn't great.'*

# GROWING UP

In contrast to other autists, I was incredibly active and present when I was a child. I chatted a lot, asked for a lot of attention, asked many questions, and loved to be in the centre of attention. In primary school I was pretty good at learning, but during my secondary education it became more difficult. I was bullied a lot, and I see that period as a black page in my life. People bullied me with my tics – which are due to my Tourette's – but later on I discovered that people picked on me because I behaved differently, and now I realise that those behavioural differences were typically autistic. I wrote a bit on this in the preface; the harassment of my childhood has stuck with me all these years.

Karen:
*'I didn't have any connection with either classmates or teachers. I was silent, I didn't say a word. During breaks I sat separately from everybody else. Reading and language in general went pretty well for me; calculus was a disaster. I think I might have dyscalculia. The advice I received for secondary education was lower vocational education, but from a more detailed test it appeared that I could reach much higher. I hated school. "They don't know what to do with you," my mother used to say.*

*I was invited for birthday parties twice per year: once by the church minister's daughter, and once by her bosom friend. Because they felt sorry for me, I bet. My mother never let me throw parties, because my birthday was during the summer holidays. It didn't occur to her that I might as well throw it on another date.*

*I went to dance classes; I did two courses. I always was left till last, and never got picked out to be in a group.'*

Natasja:

*'What I remember from preschool is that I always looked at the others, and wondered how they did all of the things they were doing – making friends and all. Eventually I had my first school friend only in the third year of secondary school. I must say that I really worked hard for that as well. She was the one who showed interest in me (which was very surprising to me), and I tried to respond to it as well as I could. Unfortunately our friendship faded out after school.'*

Sandra:

*'I was – and still am – very changeable. In school I was incredibly quiet, shy, and withdrawn, but I could be very actively present in places where the atmosphere was nice. At home, I was all but quiet. That led to certain false conclusions with regard to my behaviour at school; I must be playing the part of a shy and quiet girl in school, if I was the polar opposite at home.*

*I did go to birthday parties, but nobody liked it. I was bullied terribly. My mother said I had to throw parties, and the girls who came to my parties would tell me they had to go because their mothers had told them to. Afterwards, my mother would say how nice the parties were, and that she really liked the girls as well. But she didn't believe me when I said that it was a little bit different when she wasn't looking.*

*My mother wanted me to take dance classes when I was a teenager, because that would allegedly be very good for me. Luckily I was no longer that easy to manipulate, and I didn't do it. I was still teased, had difficulty moving around (bad mobility skills; my body awareness wasn't good, and I didn't know how exactly I related to my physical environment – I still don't). Above all, I was everything but the girl a boy would like to be seen with. It would have been a humiliating experience, and I'm happy I wasn't forced.*

*I was into gymnastics until I was about fifteen. So was the girl who teased me from primary school on, and who turned all the girls against me. She also went to the same secondary school. I was done with it all, I wanted to stop going, but every single time my mother told me that it wasn't possible, because she had already paid. In our household, money was scarce, and as such sacred. But Sandra turned fifteen and just didn't go anymore. End of story.*

*Things were getting better when I started on my vocational training (Welfare Studies). I made some friends there, I was a bit weird – though not quiet at all – and I belonged to a group. By the way, I never understood that I was accepted into the study programme, so I went to a teacher who was in the admissions committee. He told me that there had been a lot of discussion, but that he saw potential in me – and that I had widely exceeded their expectations. However, due to several circumstances things went downhill when I started to go to school there. Things weren't too great with my family situation, and that is when I had my first burn-out – although it's never been officially diagnosed as such.'*

# HYPERSENSITIVE / INSENSITIVE

I don't know whether being oversensitive is something typical to ASD, but I definitely fall under the category of people who start crying when someone says 'boo'. I am much too sensitive on many areas. Others can easily hurt me, for example, and I have enough teardrops to shed. They never really stop.

A recent example: last week, one of my neighbours called my dog 'mangy mutt', because Daisy tends to bark when she walks by with her dog. I let her have it verbally, so I seemed very assertive, but people don't see me crying on the sofa when I'm back home.

When I was a child the novel Nobody's Boy (aka Alone in the World) always made me cry, and I genuinely worried about the hungry children in Africa. I'm also bad with aggression, both to me and to others. I'll withdraw when I'm faced with it; it really leaves scars.

Many people with ASD seem insensitive, or are portrayed as such. This is often due to the fact that they can't express their feelings properly. Some people with ASD find it hard to reach their feelings, and other can't do it at all.

Anne:
*'Naturally, my emotions are pretty bland. Or, well, that's how it used to be when I was a little, naïve girl. But I'm still never very happy, or very sad, or very angry. It's always just a little. It's pleasant for me, but frustrating for others. My personal coach said that she'd be happy for me if I would break something out of anger. When I feel something, the feeling is there, but I don't*

know how to express it, or you just won't notice it about me. I had to laugh once and I happened to look in the mirror at the same time, but I saw hardly any difference with my normal face! I wasn't aware of that at all.'

Kimberley:

'I'm often seen as insensitive and indifferent. Surprisingly enough, it's mainly my mother who experiences me like that, even though she is the one who knows me best. I have a lot of difficulty expressing emotions, and hardly ever do it when people are around. When I was in my final year of secondary school, one of my teachers passed away. My mother asked me if I was doing okay under the circumstances, and I said I was – but I felt terrible. I couldn't say yes at that time, because I would start crying uncontrollably, and I don't want to do that when others are around. I can show empathy when someone is enthusiastic about something, but when someone is sad I don't know what to do. I block at those moments, and don't know what to say. Nevertheless, I do really understand that the person is sad and I feel with them; I just can't express it.

To answer the question, if I know autists who are insensitive; I don't dare to judge that. People see me as an insensitive autist, but I know I'm not. How can I judge other people with ASD, when it might work the same for them as it does for me?'

Karen:

'I'm often seen as very down to earth. I don't cry when someone dies. Their body doesn't really mean anything to me; it's just a thing lying on a bed. I miss the person who died when there's a moment we would normally be in contact, but he or she isn't there anymore.

*I hardly every show my emotions. I don't want others to see them, because I don't want them to respond. I find it difficult enough to make sense of them myself.'*

Sandra:

*'I don't like to show emotions that make me vulnerable, although there have been people with whom I am able to do that. Whether it is really due to my autism or my life's course and upbringing, I don't know. The way I was brought up definitely shaped me a lot in that respect. In our house, you had better not be too vulnerable, and during my teenage years I secluded myself. People who don't know me well tend to think I'm very down to earth.*

*I also don't like to watch the news – all those horrors hurt me. I let it get to me too much. I'll usually stick to the children's news broadcast, where it's less harsh, but still fair. And the internet, because I find text less intrusive than images.*

*I must say that this hasn't always been the case; for a very long time I've locked myself away and reasoned my way out of my emotions. I found it difficult to get to the core of what I was feeling, and this has only been a recent development.*

*I don't believe I really know people with ASD who are insensitive. I do know that they are so taken by their own head and thoughts that there simply isn't space for anyone else's. Everything you say will start a reasoning and association based on one detail of what you just said. You'll miss the reciprocity, but I don't think it is insensitivity.'*

Natasja:

*'I don't know autists who don't feel anything, but I do know other variants of not feeling. Think of not feeling anything with*

*dramatic situations, but not being able to reach your feelings with the small things, or having a delay in when you feel something, or repressing it, or simply not recognising it.'*

Hans:

*'I am one for feelings, but I also like to reason about things. And in some moments (my dad passing away) I can even surprise myself with my lack of that emo-nonsense.*

*I'm not aware of bodily oversensitivity. Maybe rather a bit of insensitivity, because I haven't worn a jumper in years, regardless of the weather. I'll wear a winter coat over my T-shirt at most.*

*I think that there are people with ASD with whom the internal emo-stuff is such a mess, that they can only trust their common sense, and would benefit most from reasoning and figuring everything out with logic (like a true Vulcan).'*

*When it comes to clothing, I only have a couple of items that I really feel comfortable in. I'm hypersensitive to certain fabrics I really can't touch, tags that cut into my skin, or fabrics that give me rashes. My skin really can't bear those micro-fibre cleaning cloths. It makes my skin prickly, and I can't stand that.*

*Many people with autism will respond hypersensitively or insensitively to their medication. I've taken valerian once, or something plant-based that was supposed to calm you down. It made me incredibly hyperactive! When I'm prescribed a new drug I always ask my doctor if I'm allowed to start on the lowest dosage, and take half of that. From experience I know that my side effects can be really severe.*

Karen:

*'I experienced hypomania to a small dose of paroxetine. I took*

*10 milligrams, while 20 mg is the regular minimal dosage. In blood examinations they couldn't find any significant amounts of paroxetine.*

*Now I'm on half a millilitre risperidon, which is very little. But when I stop taking it, I notice the immense effect it has on me. According to my psychiatrist, I respond to homeopathic dosages.'*

Sandra:

*'I respond to my medication very unpredictably. I also have half a millilitre of risperidon a day, and I'm happy to finally have found a drug that works. I'll take the side effects for granted; it makes me sleep badly (which apparently is atypical). Oxazepam can make me hyperactive.*

*I have to watch out with the use of antidepressants; they can be very harmful to me. I can't have a GP prescribe them to me; I need a psychiatrist who is willing to prescribe tremendously small dosages to start with. And who has to believe me to my word when I tell him about strange side effects. When I say that mirtazapine causes me to fall down the stairs stoned out of my mind, it really is the case.*

*Prozac really made me slightly mad once. I made a complete fool out of myself at a job interview, and literally pulled through day and night. I did think I was lovely and happy, active, and creative, even intelligent! But I became very skinny, and I later learnt that the people around me thought I was very tiring.'*

# I MAGES

Many people with ASD think in images. For me, I notice it especially with the use of figurative language. A while back, I talked to someone who told me that my past isn't exactly 'a pebble in my shoe'. This immediately called to my mind a little rock inside my shoe. I have this more often; it happens because I take expressions literally (see chapter 'Literal' for more on this). Luckily I was able to snap out of it quickly and replied, 'It probably is more like a brick!' Afterwards I couldn't help but think (I'm not even kidding): of course that isn't possible. I couldn't possibly fit a brick in my shoe.

A fellow-autist told me that, in school, he used to have trouble with word problems in maths. Some question could be about a train that left at seven o'clock. He would immediately envisage a train and diverge off track, as a result he forgot the initial math problem.


Sandra:
*'Often, my picture-thinking is on a roll during conversations. I very much like figurative use of language, such as proverbs, and I understand them entirely, but I do literally see people literally jumping the gun or breaking a leg. Such images remain for a while, during which the conversation continues. At that stage I have to fill in some parts really quickly, because I missed them, lost in my own thought.'*

Natasja:

'I literally see a year or a week, for example. When I tell someone that something occurred in January, I'll move my hand to the place where January is in my mind. I can hardly imagine what it is like to think without seeing the words, which is supposed to be "normal".'

Kimberley:

'I find thinking in words and images rather vague. When I think, I don't see letters floating by. Does that make me a picture thinker? But I don't always see images, either, so am I not a thinker then? And what about babies? Can babies think in words when they can't read? Or are babies picture thinkers per definition? (There is a nice theory about why young children always win playing memory.)

   These terms mean hardly anything to me and I shall be glad to hear when someone can clearly explain them to me.'

Hans:

'I am quite the picture thinker as well, even though I don't see images all the time. I can imagine things easily as a kind of movie or as photographs. But that doesn't happen 'autimatically' for me.'

Khadijah:

I think in images. I just see things in front of me when I read or hear something or talk to someone. This even happens when I write. When I'm on the phone with someone and they say, 'I'm hanging up now, bye', I would see them hanging by a rope.

# IMAGINATION

Many people who suffer from ASD have a huge imagination, whereas others might have no imagination at all. A while ago, I read a book written by someone with autism. The book consists of short stories with surprising plot twists. Personally, I would never be able to write such a book, simply because I don't have enough imagination to be able to come up with similar stories.

I also find it really difficult to watch films that haven't actually happened. Sometimes I just can't get into certain things. For example, I watched The Lord of the Rings in the cinema. Everybody was lyrical about the films in the trilogy, but I didn't think highly of it at all. All these strange little creatures... what a fake movie! I do try to watch movies that are somewhat science-fictiony at times, and sometimes they're all right. A friend of mine loves these 'fake' movies, so if we are to rent a DVD it is a matter of give and take. I'd rather see a movie about something that can truly happen or already did; at least I'll be able to relate to it. I like to watch documentaries and news programmes, for instance.

When I was a child, I wasn't one for role-playing games; my lack of imagination withheld me from really participating. I would rather stick to concrete activities, such as playing with marbles, football and puzzles.

Some people with ASD are so immersed in their imagination that they can no longer distinguish what is real from what is fictional. In some cases, this can lead to a brief psychotic episode.*

Kimberley:

*'In my diagnosis report, it says that I didn't have a lot of imagination when I was a child. I disagree entirely; when I was a child I had a lot of imagination and I used to write great compositions. I actually lost that imagination somewhere in secondary school. Everything had to be based on facts, we had to include bibliographies, etc. Unfortunately I lost my last spark of imagination when I went to university.'*

Sandra:

*'I can be incredibly imaginative, but not always ad hoc. So, if I were to get an assignment to come up with something straight away, chances are that I'll just stare into the distance, and won't be able to produce anything. When there's no pressure, though, it does often work out; I can think very associatively, which you'll notice in what I come up with and in the jokes that I make. Unfortunately, in the last couple of years I feel more worn out and I kind of miss my 'old' self in that respect.'*

Karen:

*'I don't think I have a vivid imagination. People thought I did when I was a child, because I was really good at writing stories. What they didn't know, however, was that the stories I wrote were based on the many books I read during that period. I could literally quote passages from some novels by heart.'*

Hans:

*'If I want to read about the real world, I'll read a newspaper (and pretend that it describes the real world, as I struggle through propaganda and glorified press reports); if I want to see the real world, I'll look outside through the window.*

*I love to watch science fiction, fantasy, etc. I really enjoy superhero movies (mainly in the Marvel Cinematic Universe, which includes films about several superheroes that take place in the same fictional reality. This implies that characters can occur or be mentioned in separate movies, and that they can be part of the same storyline). These films work when there is a type of internal logic, and if it's followed closely. I can sympathise with these characters, even though they might not be 'real'. On DVDs, they often include behind-the-scenes documentaries, which shows the many ins and outs and details of the process of making the film. Even though people say it takes away the 'magic', it doesn't bother me at all. When a character is animated well (Gollum from The Lord of the Rings, for example), I'll still be able to enjoy the film, even if I know how the character is created.*

*I'm not that great at inventing stories. Although I can think of some scenes or some specific moments in a story, I find it difficult to create a complete story with an entire internal logic.'*

Khadijah:

*'I have so much imagination, sometimes it feels like my head's going to explode if I don't do anything with it. I love applying my imagination by writing, because I can really lose myself in my work, and I notice that I really enjoy doing it.*

*I can't imagine what it's like to live without imagination. Even though people often have thought, and still think, that I am super realistic, they have no idea of the way I think. I love losing myself in books, but writing gives me something extra; I can express the stuff I make up, reread it, and live through it.'*

*Brief psychotic episodes: during a psychosis, sufferers lose contact with reality. The processing of information has been disrupted heavily. This can become clear through delusions and/or hallucinations. During a brief psychotic episode, the sufferer is on the border of a psychosis, implying that they know that their delusions are not real.*

# INTELLIGENCE

My intelligence appears to be quite high; I once scored 135 on an intelligence test. On the one hand, I quite like it and I'm proud of it. On the other hand, it is incredibly frustrating, because I believe I should be able to understand practically everything. Unfortunately it doesn't work that way in practice. Aside from my ASD I also have ADD and Gilles de la Tourette, which combination makes it far from ideal. Sometimes I can't even come across as intelligent ;-)

This does lead people to over-estimate my capabilities; people usually think I can do most things on my own. Quite the opposite is true, though. I receive ambulatory help through a PIP, which includes domestic care. I'm also not that great at seeing the big picture of things. My personal coach helps me with my administration and helps me when I have to call agencies. I find this difficult, because conversations tend to go differently than what I anticipate, which often causes me to lose track. He helps me with this.

Of course, there are people with ASD who have a lower

intelligence; they are less likely to be overestimated in terms of capacity.

Moreover, intelligence can surface as very one-sided in people with ASD. Some people with ASD, usually men, are very intelligent when it comes to technical things, and there are others who are incredibly good at languages. Although this is a bit of a sweeping oversimplification, the point is that intelligence can out itself in many different forms.

Hans:

*'According to the WAIS-III test I once took, I have an IQ of 101 points (it's possibly a bit higher, because the tension of making the test probably influenced it). Apparently I need my intelligence so much to just get through the day that I don't see myself as intelligent. But that stops at the point when I start comparing myself to people who believe everything that's in the newspapers.*

*In the past, people thought I wasn't the brightest crayon in the box, but the same people also thought I was smart enough to do certain other things. This could be a task at my old job or another chore that didn't go too well in practice. I've also made some comments that didn't come off as too bright. 'That's a stupid remark,' people used to say. I also heard that I would be able to easily solve a problem, because I was 'clever enough to do it'. In retrospect, I realise I should've told him, 'That's not true, because I have to use my hands to do that task.'*

*I think there's an issue to take with Verbal IQ and Performance IQ; you might be able to explain a certain action very well (Verbal IQ), but to show how it is done might be a lot more difficult (Performance IQ).*

*Sometimes my head isn't quite where it should be, so I might not pay a lot of attention to conversations that are happening right in front of me. I'll respond to a part of it that I happen to catch, but it might very well be something they'd discussed a couple of minutes before ('We just talked about that; pay attention, Hans!').'*

Kimberley:
*'I think I use part of my intelligence to compensate for my ASD. I'm happy to be in this position, though. I function pretty well in general, and I use "what I have left" to learn social rules and that sort of thing. That doesn't take away the fact that I do think it's a shame I need that; on occasion it feels like I can do a lot more than what I show people.'*

Rob B:
*'I have the convenience of a considerable intelligence. It enables me to assess what I'm good at, and I'm pretty good at hiding it and compensating for it. Luckily, I'm not that intelligent that I want to solve difficult life questions. Thanks to my intelligence I can also sympathise with people (which I've been taught how to do). Actually feeling with them is a lot more difficult.'*

Karen:
*'In primary school, teachers didn't know which level I should attend. Should I go to the lowest, the highest, or something in between? I was good at some things, but terrible at other subjects.*

*Maths was, and still is, problematic. I never studied place names and countries for topography. I thought it was nonsense, because you can just take a map when you need one. Why would*

*I learn all the place names by heart? A test in my final year of primary school showed that I would be a good student for college, but I eventually would be able to do university as well, even though the school told me the opposite. The test showed that my intelligence was above average.*

*I've heard differently since then, though; people think I'm pretty intelligent, some even say I could be highly gifted. I think I'm above average, but that I appear smarter in several areas. It's probably because I have a lot of factual knowledge; I know a lot about medication, diseases, and other conditions, for instance. These things really interest me, and I run into them at work quite regularly. So that's where they think I'm clever, which is an advantage.'*

Sandra:

*'I really don't know. After my college training I started university – which I didn't finish, by the way. At that stage I received very high grades, and not everyone had that. I'm probably not that unintelligent, maybe not at all. It really opened my eyes back then. Several separate coaches have called me highly gifted as well, but I don't believe that; it doesn't appear from IQ-test scores that go paired with my diagnosis, either. That score was pretty average. Whether I'm stupid or not, I function the way I function and that probably is partly due to my intelligence, but when it comes to performance within society I don't really care much for it. I prefer not to appear all too clever, because people might have all sorts of expectations, and I simply don't understand things that quickly; I am terrible at knowing the essence of things, I forget a lot, and my attention span is incredibly bad.'*

63

# Jobs

About ten years ago, I still worked as a teacher in primary school. I am quite confident in saying that this job isn't exactly autism-proof. If there's any job where you have to multitask, it's teaching in elementary school.

The reason why I kept that job for almost ten years is because I liked it so much. At that time, I really enjoyed having children around me. Unfortunately, it already started to become too much after only two years. Long days wore me out. It happened quite frequently that I would be checking assignments at eleven at night, and I did the administration and wrote reports during the vacations. After having surgery to my eye and knee, I crashed entirely and was admitted to a psychiatric hospital as a matter of crisis. Autism wasn't a matter at hand at that stage, and neither was Tourette's syndrome. After another admission and a year of day treatment, I returned to working in primary education. I also obtained a diploma for remedial teaching, which means I'm specialised in coaching children who have problems with learning or their behaviour. With renewed enthusiasm I once again started multitasking in the job I loved so much. Unfortunately I've had to pay for this with what I call a 'chronical burn-out'. I've crossed my own boundaries so often in work situations, which left me feeling burnt out – a feeling I doubt I'll lose.

Much later, I was diagnosed with Gilles de la Tourette, and my autism diagnosis – Autism Spectrum Disorder – only came at age 39. After quite a hassle I ended up working in a nursing home, and I am very happy to work there as a host and carer. Currently

I'm working as a volunteer again; I no longer have my paid job as a result of cutbacks.

The difficult thing about having a job is that it leaves me exhausted quite quickly; discussing with people, multitasking and time pressure are all factors of stress to me. At the moment, working eight hours a week is my maximum workload.

I've seriously considered starting up my own small-scale photography business; I'm still registered with the Chamber of Commerce. I also built an entire studio where I can enjoy my work. I have a couple of jobs per year that I'll commit to completely, but the benefits of owning a business don't outweigh the drawbacks.

I already stress out when there's a stranger in my house, let alone having to do a photography job for them. The administration that is accompanied by such jobs also takes a lot of energy, and I find it difficult to have someone else do it for me. At the moment I'll only have my cat and dog to play model for me, and I'll bug the insects in my garden – but they don't put up much of a fight.

Natasja:
*'Something I would definitely want to have in a book about autism – if I were to write it myself – would be that some people are simply not capable of working. The government is all about participation and looking at what people can still do, and about making yourself helpful to society by working, and about that it's better for your self-image, etc. But this particular society is designed in such a way that it simply isn't possible for some to work. Not everyone is able to make a living.*

*I've never had a job, and I don't see it happening that I ever will. I simply can't. That is, I can't do it without breaking down entirely. As a child and teenager, I imagined myself working. I wondered how on earth I'd be able to do it, but it would all work out in the end. It ended up being completely different, though; after I stopped my study grant and didn't have any income at all, I realised that it would become very difficult. I was on the lookout for jobs where you don't need to be in contact with people all too much, because I found dealing with people very difficult and tiring. I didn't know about autism yet. I would have liked to be a shepherd, although I would be in trouble with heat outside, because I can't handle heat very well (I wouldn't be able to function). However, after I found the job requirements for shepherds, I found that one of the requirements was that you 'have to be sociable'. Apparently, shepherds have to talk to people as well.'*

Kimberley:

*'Four years ago, I started working at a store. I still work there, between three and nine hours per week. I have more hours during the summer holidays, but I would never be able to work there fulltime. The job is quite easy – it's only a simple part-time job. I do find it difficult when people say something and I take it differently, and I'm not that good at responding to annoying customers. I usually solve the latter by asking help from someone who's in charge; I'll have them fix the problem for me.'*

Sandra:

*'I don't have a job. Sometimes it's tough, because it doesn't exactly put me in a desirable position in society. I'm somewhere down below and completely dependent on the government. Added to that, I'm also a psychiatric patient, even though they came up*

*with some lovely and vague terms for that. When I tell people that I don't have a job, but that I go to a day centre, they'll often say, 'Oh! Sorry!' and they're off.*

*I think it's a pity that I can't work; I often find it hard that I'm not able to really develop myself, and that I have to do things that are below my level. I really have to make sure that I don't put too much of my energy in it, because that would be a shame. However, I have no idea how I would survive if I had a job. I am tired pretty often, much more so than the people around me might notice. Only people close to me will know about it. Everyday activities take up a lot of energy. Doing the groceries is a tough task – I'm not saying I don't like it, but it is cause to over-stimulation. Sadly, it isn't something that just passes.*

*Other than that, my family also takes up a lot of time. I'm very quick to cancel my appointments with the day centre for them. Doing that isn't always the best choice, not even for me, but I'm happy to not have to split myself into two, as it were. I won't have to feel guilty. And when I'm too tired at the day centre, I just say that I'll go home earlier during that day, and just leave early. I could choose to go only on the more calm days, and avoid over-stimulation. I don't have to pretend to be flexible, or not at day centre, anyway (although I will pose to be more flexible than I feel sometimes; I'm used to that). I can just say to a coach, "I understand this might seem odd to you, but I can't really do anything right now". I just find it difficult to learn new things. Tell that to your boss – they want efficiency. "Sorry, boss, I know I have to learn what to do on my own, but please just tell me what to do. Oh, and I also apologise in advance for forgetting the first sentence when you start on the second, when you explain something. And, yes, I already forgot that I would do X, and I'm ashamed to admit that I also forgot to do Y."*

*When I did have a job, it wore me out so much that it drove me to illness. I already had the flu before they found the virus, as it were. There wasn't really time to recover for a couple of weeks; I did it, but I was always required back too early. I just wasn't fully recovered by that time, and yet I'd have to go back to work. Before I knew it, I was working with a 40-degree fever again. I became more ill and depressed, I really wanted to work, but I only failed. Then you're out on the streets again.*

*Not to mention the social stuff that comes with having a job. I just can't do it, the social pressure, competition, scheming, etc. How do I deal with that? Some colleagues were nice, and I'd become friends with them, but I've always been the odd one out and that creates suspicion. Miscommunications happened every day and didn't exactly help.'*

Hans:

*'I've had a job for years, and was referred to as 'perfect employee' at my previous job. Every colleague had to work the way I did. I knew the most and I knew how to solve nearly every problem. That is, until there were more tasks to the job, and I began to lose track. New methods were instated by management, even though we – the people who had to do the actual work – knew how to do it more efficiently. Protesting didn't work, though. Eventually I ended up with a nervous breakdown (although it's never officially been called a burnout). During this time, I also was diagnosed with autism. By now I'm quite glad to have quit working. Having experienced how ill I become when I do something outside of the day-centre environment, I know that I was rightfully judged as entirely unfit for work.*

# KIDDING

I feel like my fellow autists should say 'just kidding' more often than anyone, because they are the most humorous people walking the face of the earth. To 'prove' this, I picked a couple of fragments from the aforementioned forum of which I'm an administrator. Although not everyone may have written something that was meant to be funny, these fragments did make me smile, which is why I've put them in.

Read and judge for yourself:

Karen (filed under 'What did you do today, or what are you going to do?'):
*'Worked, sleeped, laptopped, walked, groceried, cooked, eated, dishwashed, and laptopped again.'*

Marc:
*'Good evening. Today was a bit of a boring day. I'm going to leave the computer the computer for a while. Good night.'*

Yentl:
*'Good evening. Today was a little bit of a boring day.*
*I'm going to let my computer out. Sweet dreams, for now. Let out... I read it differently :-)'*

Sandra:
*'Letting out the computer, haha! It would be typically me, having my computer on wheels on a leash, pulling it behind me. And, when it growls to a person, say: It normally never does this!'*

Karen:
*'Haha, another one! You can probably paste Sandra in your book. She really has a sense of humour.'*

Natasja:
*'Then they wouldn't even be able to close the book!'*

\* \* \*

During a game of Wordfeud:
Isa:
*'Very well-found!!'*

Marc:
*'I thought 'geeksome' was well-found as well, Isa. Idea for a modern fairy tale? Little Geeksome Riding Hood?'*

Isa:
*'Haha, I sense a story emerging!'*

Marc:
*'Once upon a time, Little Geeksome Riding Hood was playing games on her little tablet. One day, she went into the Geeky forest and ran into the wolf named Google.'*

\* \* \*

Sandra:
*'I really don't understand dates. Sitting somewhere with someone you don't know, apart from sending some emails, wearing clothes you normally never wear and try to be as nice*

*as you can. A type of job interview. And both of the two falling for that trap. No, I'll stay away from dating.'*

Khadijah:

*'A date is just an appointment, it can also just be with someone you know or a friend. A blind date is with someone you don't know.*

*And whether or not you're dateable, that's determined by your calendar and enthusiasm, not your weight.'*

\* \* \*

Karen:

*'The Easter eggs from the supermarket break in half differently than they did in the previous years. Usually they were two halves, but now they break on the thin side. Does it still make sense to you?'*

Kimberley:

*'That's annoying, about those Easter eggs! I always bite them in half first (that is, over the long side) and then I eat both halves separately (Me, autistic? Where do you get that idea?)'*

\* \* \*

Anna:

*'I feel a little down. I have no idea what caused my sadness. It's so typical. Can anyone say something funny? I might be able to start laughing without stopping. Preferably as loud as possible, to make the Big Ben shake, but if you can put a simple smile on my face, that's good enough as well!'*

# Literal Meanings

Many people with ASD take language literally. There also are those who take it literally, but are able to switch so quickly that they don't interpret it literally. I myself have had to learn how to do this to communicate better and easier.

Something I still very clearly remember from my time in teacher training is a first-aid exam. We had a victim who had to play that she had a plaster's angle in her arm, and I was supposed to help her. I wanted to start by taking the angle out, when I realised that there wasn't an actual thing in her arm... It just was an ugly wound that needed taking care of. I was embarrassed when I found out, but luckily I passed the exam.

In my experience, by taking something literally, the person's utterance is no longer valid. Take, for instance, when someone says, 'I am speechless', and then they elaborate on why exactly they are speechless and how they feel. This happens a lot on TV. I'll think to myself, 'Wow, you're so speechless, that makes so much sense!' (Sarcastically, of course.) Another example of something I take literally is user manuals, but that isn't necessarily a bad thing.

A while back, I bought a cherry pit pillow – one of those pillows you can heat up in the microwave, to heat muscles in your back and neck to drive away the pain. The packaging says that you should put it in the microwave for no longer than two minutes. I was talking to a friend about the pillow, and she says she always heats it for four minutes. I blurted out, 'But you're not allowed to do that, right?' She replied that it won't be warm enough for her taste. For some reason, I simply hadn't realised that it was possible to put it in the microwave longer, even though I already thought it cooled down pretty quickly.

I've improved in following recipes when cooking. I'll still keep an eye on the time, but I also taste regularly to see if the food is done yet.

Kimberley:
*'I take language more literally than I thought I did. The director of my orchestra told me once that he didn't dare to tell me when to play a part a bit more slowly. I always take what he says too literally. I tend to overcompensate; when it's supposed to be slower, I don't slow down a little bit, but a lot. I also see the literal meaning of something that's being said, first and only after that the non- literal meaning – the way it is intended. Now, I'm usually able to respond when I know what is meant, and I don't go off on my first hunch. I used to respond immediately, which could lead to strange and awkward situations.'*

Rob B:
*'Through experience I know that much of what people say is not meant literally. Knowing that I shouldn't take things literally is pretty well-integrated in my system by now. Taking something literally is, however, can be quite funny; when there's an expression that I can actually see happening, you might find me chuckling every once in a while.'*

Hans:
*'My first thought when it comes to an expression or something else non-literal is the literal meaning of the phrase. Usually I'm quite quick in translating it to what is actually meant.*
*I don't always notice if I'm translating, though; I'll smirk at a*

*literal interpretation. This also is a source of being funny for me, but puns and other language jokes aren't always appropriate for every audience, who might look at me strangely (What do you mean? What are you talking about?).*

*When I'm tired, stressed, or generally not feeling well (even though my fingers are perfectly operational), the translation usually takes a bit longer. It's clear that I'll have to take things slow at that moment. I'm very likely to respond to the literal meaning of something in all seriousness, before I come to realise that something else is probably meant.'*

Sandra:
*'Pretty often, I'll see things in front of me quite literally, but usually I won't actually understand it as such. I might make jokes about the literal interpretation, which may also cause problems when the person I'm talking to also thinks as literally and doesn't get the joke. And that is how misunderstandings are brought about.*

*A while back I had a conversation with someone, who asked if I wanted to talk about something "now". "Well," I said, "Let's do it after we're done swimming. 'Now' is a bit difficult, since we are busy with this at the moment." Then it appeared that by "now" he meant "later". He wanted to discuss it after swimming.'*

# Motor skills

Many people with ASD have difficulties with their motor skills, because they aren't always as well-developed. I am of the opinion that it can be trained to a certain extent, but it will take a lot of effort. In primary school I had trouble with writing; my parents helped me with that. Through a lot of practice I've improved the neatness of my writing, but I can very well remember the time before I developed an intelligible handwriting of my own. Your own handwriting has to be pretty, but you also have to be able to take notes quickly.

During teacher training we also had to practice our sewing skills; I thought that was absolutely horrible. I couldn't get the thread through the eye of the needle, let alone doing embroidery. Crochet, knitting, embroidering... those activities weren't for me. As an adult I've knitted some scarfs with thick needles, though. Especially my fine motor skills could do with some refinement.

In sports, however, I was lucky to belong to one of the better ones. I think this makes me an exception to other people with ASD. I also liked exercise and was in good shape. However, keeping the insight in a game remained difficult. Many autists were picked last for teams in PE class. I really hope teachers have changed the ways of forming groups – having children pick their classmates always leads to these embarrassing and frustrating moments. I've been engaged with sports all my life. I still climb indoors every week with a couple of climbing buddies.

Hans:

*'I was terrible at PE, and especially at team sports. I didn't understand how other people could just understand one another, but that's probably to do with Theory of Mind [see chapter 'Theory'].*

*When it comes to motor skills, I'm a bit stiffer when I'm stressed or panicked, or something alike. Normally I don't really feel stiff, but I suspect I walk a lot more stiffly than I think I do.'*

Sandra:

*'My body awareness isn't that good. Of course, I know where all the parts are (limbs, head, etc.), but the exact fine tuning isn't sufficient. This makes my movement stiff, my handwriting irregular, and it also makes me less suitable for activities that require fine motor skills. When I was a child I was one of those glue monsters, who used too much glue and handed in gloopy messes that passed for art. I could do a bit of embroidery (when I was a bit older), but free embroidery became too messy. I was, however, good at Ministeck puzzles.*

*Because of my badly tuned motor skills, I find it difficult to place myself properly within a group or a space. I also find it hard to dodge or catch objects that move towards me. If you like slapstick comedy, you should see me play tennis. After the ball bounces I've lost it. I'm also not that good at aiming.*

*Team sports require insight, quick response in a changing situation. You have to be able to anticipate, and at that stage I'm still working out what's going on around me [detail perception; the puzzle pieces], so it is difficult to be ahead of the situation. And guess who always was chosen last and with a deep sigh in PE? By the way, these things don't just go for sports situations, but also lead to dangers in traffic; I can't learn how to drive a car, and I'll run into tables more easily than others would. Moreover, my attention span also prevents me from keeping my head with the game or the traffic or the conversation.'*

Hans:
*'A couple of fragments of memories: I once stood in the living room looking at my parents, and I wondered, 'Who are these people?' Through reasoning (I look like my brother, so we must be family; my brother looks a lot like my aunt, so they are family; and my aunt looks like my father, so they are family as well), I had to figure out that I was related to my father, and I assumed that I was related to my mother as well, so I hadn't been adopted.*

*I had moments before where I looked in the mirror, or looked at my hands, and wondered who that person staring back at me was. Maybe it's a lack of body awareness? I don't really have this anymore, though.'*

Marc:
*'The words "motor skills" were overused during my childhood. My parents whined about it constantly; they took everything the doctors and educationalists said for truth, and apparently they thought it was very interesting. How autistic. I'm blaming it on my bad concentration.'*

# NEUROTYPICAL

Neurotypical, or NT for short, is the term for everyone with an 'ordinary' neurological and psychological development in the brain. For neurotypical people, the development in the areas of processing and using social and sensory information is considered 'normal' and 'adapted'. In short: neurotypicals are 'normal' people.

A website describes the neurotypical syndrome as a neurobiological disorder, which is characterised by
• Preoccupation with social concerns
• Delusions of superiority
• Obsessions with conformity
Mind: this definition is taken from the satirical Institute for the Study of the Neurologically Typical.

Fellow autists often tell me that they wouldn't want to be NT at all. When I look at myself, there are a couple of NT traits that I don't have but would like to possess. In general, I'd like to be able to understand people better. I find that there's a lot of communication going on between the lines, and I really don't understand how some NTs can understand something when I don't. Something I would also like, since I'm sharing my wishes anyway, is a resistance to stimuli. I'm talking about noises, smells, images, and commotion around me.

As for the rest, I don't really feel connected with the 'common folk', so to speak. I only take part in fashion when I like it; I would love to talk about my dog Daisy all day, every day; I love to walk for hours with my camera to snap a picture of an insect; and I hate it when people don't live up to their agreements, make empty promises, or lie. I can keep going like this for a while. (Of course, you won't need to have ASD to agree with me here.)

Kimberley:
*'I wouldn't necessarily want to be NT. Sometimes I can enjoy the little things, and I think that part of that is due to my ASD. Simple things make me happy: the sun shining brightly, the birds singing, the flowers, when a pet sits next to me, etc. People don't always understand that.*

*Something I would really like to be able to do is having successful conversations. Knowing how to respond to what people say. That is what I find the hardest, but I also have someone to help me with it.*

*Behaviour that annoys me – but that isn't restricted to neurotypicals – is that people are so quick in judging one another. In my orchestra, for instance, there's a guy who very obviously has ASD. He behaves 'strangely', and people laugh and make fun of him behind his back, even though he can't help it.'*

Sandra:
*'My autism can make me very happy, yet at the same time extraordinarily sad. I can enjoy observations, the sun on my skin, the wind in my hair, something nice someone does for me, my children, and my pets. If I'd have to trade in my autism and lose that, I would miss it a lot. On the other hand, I'm also very easily touched by something sad, for instance. I don't have that thick of a skin.*

*However, if being NT means being less isolated, being better at making contact, and being able to connect to people easier, I would probably be less unhappy. At least, that's what I imagine it to be like. But the grass will always look greener on the other side. I can appear very sociable, but it is only in the exception when I can really make a connection. I don't know if it's just the autism that is in the way of accomplishing that, though. I can't quite put my finger on it.*

*When I'm amongst people, I often feel lonelier than when I'm alone, because I'm confronted with my being different. It's quite a struggle most of the time, because I don't want to be alone all the time. Sometimes I consider cancelling day centre to not be confronted with this fact continuously. Perhaps it would help if I were to become less conscious of my being different; I'd only have to put that aside instead of my entire autism. But, well, I'd probably miss that, too. ;-)'*

Marc:

*'As neurotypical, I would probably be able to work my way through a better education, I wouldn't have to watch every penny, and I wouldn't feel like the national government's toy. And then I wouldn't have had the entire relationship-soap. But what good would that do? That's not how it is. And I have a pretty good life in other areas.'*

# ODD

Being diagnosed with ASD, you simply are different than other people. I know people who have been called odd, crazy, strange, weird and worse. Funnily enough, I am of the opinion that it's the people around me who are different. Why would I be called 'different'? Simply because I belong to a smaller group, a group of people who have ASD? In my opinion, the bigger group, the ones without ASD, is similarly different.

It's the same with homosexuality. A smaller group of people is attracted to the same sex, so they are called 'gay' for convenience. But who is to say that the bigger group shouldn't be called something different? In the same way applied to autism, why would the bigger group not be called ASD?

To put it according to social measures: according to the guidelines, *I* am 'odd'.

# PRECISION

This is perhaps one of the most important things for people with ASD. Don't beat around the bush, just say exactly what you mean. My first coach once said, 'I should probably leave around four o'clock.' That didn't work for me. 'What time do you have to leave?' I asked. The word 'probably' is used far too often, in my opinion. It can really confuse life.

I like metaphors, but it takes too much energy to follow them and 'translate' them to my own world. Therapists are really good at using them. But I prefer them just telling me how things are, because I don't need a metaphor.

I had, and still have, some trouble with friendships that just fade out. Why can't someone simply say why they no longer want to be in contact? By now I've learnt that this is just the way things happen, and that I do the same thing on occasion. However, when someone asks me why, I will answer in all honesty.

Something that also gives me a lot of stress is when people don't live up to what they say. When someone says they're coming over at two o'clock, I'll be ready to receive them at a quarter to two. But when it's past two, I'll start to stress out a little. And when they're still not there at a quarter past two, I can hardly calm my nerves. It's much easier when they just send a message saying they'll be a bit later. But even then it's difficult, because I have no idea what 'a bit later' means exactly.

I know that I can't expect others to completely adapt to my little world, but it remains difficult.

Hans:

'Yes, it is very important to be precise. When communication is plain, it doesn't even matter what the content of the message is; I can handle personal criticism better when it's obvious what it means. When I agree with their feedback, I can work with it; when I disagree, I find it easy to just let it go. There are enough people whose communication is really vague, because they claim to not be able to do otherwise, or because they have a hidden agenda. They'll ask how you're doing, and already have a follow-up question ready on the basis of your answer. My previous boss was one of those people; he only was interested in you when he wanted something from you.'

Kimberley:

'I really need clarity. When something is unclear, I'll keep asking until I have something I can work with. When I was a child, my parents could never take me somewhere spontaneously; I always precisely wanted to know where we were going and how long we would be staying. I still want to know these sorts of things now, but I'm better at handling uncertainty. I try to be more flexible and to just let things happen. Sometimes I succeed, sometimes I don't.

For me, it's very important to have the general schedule of my week. I plan things per week, and I want everything to be in my planning. I can't adjust it. This means that I can't set appointments in the same week, because then my schedule will be off. When I set out to do something and I don't know how long it'll take exactly, I use reasoning to try and figure out how much time something will cost, or I just don't plan anything after it.

It differs per situation what happens when someone isn't precise or something isn't clear. I won't get a meltdown – at *least, not visibly. It works introspectively for me: I tend to get restless and nervous. Sometimes I'll ask questions obsessively, which is something that other people dislike. That often causes unpleasant situations. People grow angry with me or respond being impatient or irritated, even though I'm only trying to get a clear picture.'*

# QUEST

It was only at age 39 that my quest for the right diagnosis was complete. On the Tourette forum I found some people who had ASD-diagnosis, which got me thinking. I didn't really believe that I only had Tourette's; the way I perceive things is so much different from people on the forum. Something I also noticed was that autism is quite prevalent within my family, both on my mother's and on my father's side. I've been tested for ASD on multiple occasions, but I later read the reports. 'Client makes eye contact,' which I did, because that's what I'd learnt. That's what you're supposed to do, right?

Eventually I went to a general psychiatric establishment that also specialised in women with ASD. After an entire afternoon of talking, we finally concluded I had Asperger's, ASD. They also detected ADD, which didn't surprise me at all. Funnily enough, I was relieved and quite happy, because I finally knew why people always thought I was so 'weird'. Events from the past fell into place, such as making and retaining friends. It had been so difficult throughout my life, and now I understood that my ASD had part in that as well. Luckily it's also gone well for me; I have a couple of friends for over twenty years now. It isn't always me breaking contact, though; not everyone thinks my ASD and I are easy to deal with, and they'll simply end our friendship. Also, as I said before, I require help for the organisation of my administration and household, and my diagnosis made it easier to get the right help.

Sandra:

*'I was diagnosed when I was 41, that's four years ago. Before my diagnosis I had a sense that I had something, but the assistance wasn't quite there yet. Autism in a woman, who is not mentally handicapped, who is not a child, and who runs a household by herself. Obviously, there are some ideas surrounding autism that don't apply to me (or at least not at first sight). These prejudices are present amongst social workers as well, and the psychiatrist literally laughed in my face and started to lecture me that autism didn't exist.*

*When it came to my case, they thought more in the direction of borderline, and the rest was all caused by youth traumas and other traumatic experiences. I won't deny that they don't play a part – they colour me as much as my autism does – but I really don't have borderline. After whining a lot I finally succeeded in having myself tested again, and it turned out that I have ADD. You could do those questionnaires online a well, it wasn't that extensive. But, nevertheless, that was more in the direction that I was aiming for, and I still agree with the diagnosis. It offered some grip to me, and that's something that autists can work with.*

*Even later again, during day treatment, I did find some support, and even later, after a complete admission, I decided that I needed some diagnostics in that area to understand myself and be able to find more specific help. Eventually I was finally, officially an autist.*

*The first thing I felt was relief. I allowed myself to set the bar lower now, reassess my expectations of the future, and show people what exactly I had trouble with. I could finally admit to myself that I wasn't overreacting, that I wasn't just whiny, that I did take responsibility. Above all, this diagnosis made me feel stronger against the comments of people who like to simplify things in life and blamed me for it. It felt like my honour was restored.*

*I didn't get any assistance, though; after the fifteen-minute diagnostic interview I was outside with a new label. Luckily, however, there are loads of forums and hands-on experts. An intense period of self-examination ensued. Many people who were diagnosed on later age see their entire life come by, and start to place everything in the perspective of autism. That's exactly what happened to me.*

*But it wasn't just a blessing; it was a sentence as well. It would never go away. I started to see problems I faced in relationships from a different angle. It doesn't make it easier to come into contact with new people; quite the contrary. I was always aware that I was different, and I only notice this more now. Who knows how this will develop; write another book in ten years, and I'll tell you how things have changed!'*

# RIGID

The majority of the people with ASD I know are pretty rigid or obstinate in the way they think. I am part of this group. However, the older I become, the more I notice that I'm more open towards other people's opinions. That doesn't mean it's easy; quite the contrary, because sometimes I simply don't understand why someone else can take a point of view that I can't take. I know they do see things differently, but I just don't understand why. The most difficult thing is when there's hardly any logic to their principles.

For example, I would rather bankrupt myself than abandon one of my pets. I don't understand how other people think otherwise... Or when people have their pets put down when they don't have money for an operation. That sort of thing can really anger me. Sometimes it's difficult for the people around me, because they are the ones who have to deal with my moodiness.

When I was a teenager, this really was difficult for me. I used to dump my opinion with so much conviction that I didn't make myself popular with classmates. Later, when I did teacher training, I remained the colleague who dared share her deviant opinion. This is also partly due to my strong sense of justice, which I've always had. When something happens that's unjust, I will fight against it, even if it means that I stand alone in this battle.

In the past I've done some volunteer work for an older lady. She was a bit cranky, and she would always complain when I'd done groceries. She made me feel like I couldn't do anything right. I then decided that I'm not made for working with the elderly. This was an opinion I held for quite some time, until I started working in a nursing home a couple of years ago. A world opened up to me: these people were so grateful! It really is the best job I've had.

Sandra:

'Yes, I'm quite obstinate. I don't want to be, but, because of my fragmented thinking and being so strongly focused on one aspect, I can find it quite difficult to see other sides to something, or different views on something. How strong this feeling is also depends on the people and situations; when I'm relaxed I will have more space to think otherwise, so to speak. Or when people tell me, "But you can also think about it like this, or like that." Oh, right! I also like to say, "Me? Obstinate? Noooo, absolutely not! Props to the person who can convince me otherwise!"'

89

# STIMULI

This chapter isn't about what excites people, but about the effects of sounds, images, and other things that can really get to people with ASD. 'We' like to call this becoming over-stimulated. Like everybody else, I can stand noises better at one moment than at another. But I do think that my senses are developed more strongly or differently than those of neurotypicals.

For example, the people who live six houses next to me own a parrot. Their animal drives me insane sometimes, even though he's not always outside. But when their back door is open, and so is mine, I can hear him and that stresses me out. It ruins my garden-fun time on occasion. I'll bet my hat that most of the people who live near don't even know there is a parrot around.

Something else I remember pretty well: I was on holiday in the Cariban with a fellow autist. We had a small studio with a terrace. Every day, from early morning till halfway in the afternoon our peace and quiet was interrupted by a sanding machine. On the opposite side of the road, they were doing a renovation for which they needed one. It drove us insane. Eventually we asked the neighbour if she didn't mind the noise; she hadn't even noticed the damn thing. After listening carefully, she finally heard that it did indeed make quite some noise.

When I'm in a car with someone who has their music on, I ask if they can turn it down a bit, or preferably off entirely. My head feels like it's going to explode within a few minutes, especially when I also want to keep up a conversation with them.

By way of comparison: go and sit in a shaft with subwoofers all around you, the bass as loud as it can, and the volume as high as possible, and keep this up for a few minutes. Neurotypicals might think this situation is absurd, but this is what it feels like to me when I'm in a car with a radio at 'normal' volume, and where it is 'expected' to still be able to have a conversation.

I also don't really like shopping, unless I'm the only person in the store. I often get dizzied by all the people walking around in the store, and all the noises I hear I can't handle people bumping into me either. This unexpected physical contact really over-stimulates me.

Natasja:
*'When I'm over-stimulated I have difficulty sleeping, no matter how tired I am. My head is so clouded, everything needs to be pre-processed before I can process it in my sleep. I've had trouble sleeping since I was little.'*

Rob B:
*'Sometimes I think it's an amazing sensation to get over-stimulated completely. When there's one day in which I see too much, do too much, experience too much, but all of which I enjoy immensely. I don't mind if it means that I'll have to catch my breath for the next few days.'*

Kimberley:
*'I get over-stimulated quite quickly. Especially when there's noise and when many people are around me (which also produces quite some sound ;-)). Yes, I am a member of a music association – two, actually. And, no, I don't mind the noise, although I do play with earplugs in my ears at one group. Music*

*is 'organised' sound, there's logic to it. What bothers me most is monotonous sounds, such as cars driving at idle speed, but I can deal with the sound of clocks. The very worst is the sound that is continuous but outside of my control. Sometimes the neighbours put on their music so loudly that I can literally hear the lyrics. These things can lead to crying fits, because I really can't handle that. I also get this when my brother is playing a computer game with sirens.*

*Having many people around me also leads to over-stimulation, but I can't pinpoint why exactly that is. Too many people produce too much of everything. Both visually and auditory, but also tactile – when they bump into you – and even smells can work against me. When I'm in a crowd of people for too long, I'll start looking at it in fragments. That's what you see in all those instructional videos about ASD: people are unable to see a room as a whole, but on detailed level.*

*And that's one of the most threatening things for me, because I'll become over-stimulated and consequently unable to communicate.*

*I'm not (yet) good enough at preventing over-stimulation. I try to find ways to help myself, to be able to calm down on busy days. I still haven't figured out how to do that best. I'll usually try to get as much rest as I can on busy days, but that doesn't always work out. On Saturday, for instance, I had a competition, and I was over-stimulated afterwards. Luckily we got home at a quarter past one at night, so I could go straight to bed. The next day I had to work, and at the end of the day I wasn't able to do anything anymore. In two weeks I have another competition, but I've asked the day after off this time, so I can 'de-stimulate'. Sometimes it also helps to withdraw to the dressing room on days like those, just to have no people around.'*

# STRUCTURE

Structure is an incredibly important thing in my life, but unfortunately I'm not always able to create it. Luckily, I have an amazing dog who does this for me. The fact that she lives with me and that I have to take care of her already gives me a structure. I walk her at least three times a day, and I get a lot of love in return. What else could a person want?

Other structures in my routine are the climbing nights on Tuesday, my volunteer work on Thursday evening, and a visit to my parents every other week. Apart from that, I don't have a fixed time to eat, a fixed time to go to bed – although I always try to be in bed before twelve – and my dog adapts to my walking schedule, which changes every day. When I think about doing it, I put my appointments in an appointment book, and scribble things I shouldn't forget (nearly unintelligibly) on a whiteboard in the room. There is hardly any structure to the rest of it. Regardless of having tried very hard, I can't seem to structure my life properly, and miss and forget a lot as a result.

Kimberley:
*I need structure very much. I have a whiteboard, but I usually just use that as a memory aid. On it, I write things I shouldn't forget. In the kitchen we have a planning board with household chores, which says – per day – who's cooking, does the dishes, hoovers, and does the laundry. This is normally changed four times a year (when our school schedules change). It helps to keep our home nice and tidy.*

*When it comes to studying, I also have to make a planning to keep up with everything. If I don't have a planning, I don't do anything. I use a lot of colours in my schedule; everything that is set has its own colour. Courses and anything else related to university is purple, music is blue, and my job is green. I can see at once how many things I have on which day, so that I plan less on days with a lot of colour. I try to keep my planning the same each week to get into that rhythm (on Monday, for example, I work two hours for one course, two for another, and then I have a two-hour lecture).*

*I do have to admit that I have trouble keeping to my schedules. I can't know in advance how much energy I'll have, and on some days I'm just too tired to do what I should be doing. I used to make a planning which pages of which book I would read at a given moment, but I don't do that anymore. If I don't stick to that schedule my entire planning is off.'*

Hans:

*'I don't use pictos or other pictures, but I do have a couple of sheets of paper with textual clues (a weekly schedule for housekeeping, for example). But I hardly look at that, either. So, I have a weekly housekeeping schedule that I try to follow (albeit with a little bit of delay), but only when I have problems with unexpected changes – switches – I can hardly keep up with housekeeping.*

*Other than that, I try to do fixed things during the week; I go to the day centre, which I only cancel if I'm either too tired or if I have something important that week. That's only happened a couple of times in the last few years, though. When my coach is off on holiday, I prefer to have no coach at all than a replacement (this might also have to do with switching [see the next chapter]). In the past, I didn't want my coaching to be rescheduled because I couldn't handle the change, but I've made some progress in that area.*

*When I skip all of my obligations (especially those at the day centre) – without a good reason – I become more anxious, and that's something I want to avoid. That's why I do take part in activities in the day centre, even if I'm so tired I'll only stare out into blankness. At least I've gone, and that's the most important thing.'*

Sandra:
'*When there's structure to things, it prevents me from losing track of the big line in chaos. I don't have pictos, whiteboards, or other visual aids. I have used those for my children, but I'm not that good with them, and they are unsettling to my eyes. I do use a calendar and put notes on the counter; I call this my 'external hard drive', and I write my chores on them. As a memory aid, I sometimes put a cross or a word on my hand. And, obviously, I have a calendar next to the computer, and obviously I always forget bringing it. The daily routines, though, are just in my system, in my head.'*

# Switching

For me, having difficulty switching from one thing to another is related to being in my own world. When I'm watching TV and someone rings the doorbell, dropping by spontaneously, I may find it difficult to behave in a way that is socially acceptable. I'm torn from my own world by that damn doorbell, having to switch, but that takes time, and I don't have enough of it at that moment. When I open the door and someone is being spontaneous I have to work really hard to behave 'normally'. And that isn't exactly considered social or empathetic.

Most of my friends know by now that I'd rather have them phone or text me first, if they want to visit me. A friend of mine (who is also diagnosed with ASD), put a time clock on her doorbell. After seven o'clock, it won't ring anymore. I know from other autists that they hide themselves in their house, because they don't want to open the door. It causes them a lot of stress; so much that they'll even hide in the bathroom. I have the same with my phone, which rings on moments I'd rather not have it ring. Luckily I've come far enough to simply not always answer, and decide to call them back later.

Switching like this is something that happens every single day, and it makes my head spin. A good example of this is the 'going-to-bed' ritual. Stopping the thing I'm doing is the first switch. I can't just switch all of a sudden; there has to be a sort of conclusion to my activity. Concretely, this means that the TV programme has to be over, that I have to finish what I'm doing on my computer. After that, I walk the dog and do other things that are part of this ritual: taking my medication, locking the door, letting the cat and dog upstairs, brushing my teeth, putting on my pyjamas, setting my alarm clock, and I'm probably forgetting something. And there are switching moments to conquer between each of those actions as well.

Switching is also very difficult in conversations, especially when it's in a conversation with more people. In those cases, I'll often lose track of what's going on. As I've said before, that is due to the fact that I'm still focused on the last piece of information and lose track of the rest of the conversation. I don't think that there are many people who notice this, though; all of these switches happen inside my head. Something else I've noticed is that, when someone asks me something, I'll be so caught up in my own world, lost in thought, that I'll miss the question and they have to ask it again.

Hans:
*'Switching is difficult for me when there's no clear transition between something and something else. For instance, changing from one coach to another without saying goodbye, and without having the old coach introduce the new coach to me.*

*Or I might be talking to someone about something very fascinating, but the person listening to me might not think it's interesting at all... I can become quiet all of a sudden (this is where the switch happens). It's difficult, takes a lot of energy, and in many cases I can get a bit nervous when it's paired with ambiguity. Nevertheless, it isn't unconquerable.'*

Sandra:
*'I find switching difficult. It isn't easy for me to stop doing one thing and immediately start on something else. I have a 'transition ritual' between two activities: doing something on my computer. I can't walk from one conversation into another either, and when I'm doing something and someone interrupts with a question... It takes me quite a lot of energy. Especially when I had to focus, like reading. I'll be a bit vacant, don't really hear what I'm being told or asked, or respond a bit grumpily. I always tell my children, 'In five minutes, we'll... (We'll have dinner, for example).'*

# THEORIES

In the last couple of years, there has been an increase in the amount and extensiveness of psychological theories. These new insights, paired with personal experiences, give us a more complete overview of what ASD is and what characterises it.

Central Coherence Theory

This theory assumes that people with ASD are more focused on details, and for that reason have difficulty seeing something as a whole. They are unable to make something coherent out of a story or situation. It just takes more time. For people with autism, stimuli that are received in the brain through sensory perception aren't automatically linked. Consequently, they see less context, and as such less insight in the situation.

*'I went to a simple mime performance for children. I'd seen everything: the hat the male protagonist wore, how a feather swirled down onto the stage. But what the performance was about? I have no clue.'*
— Ros Blackburn

## Theory of Mind (ToM)
This theory is associated with mind reading or mind blindness. It entails that people with ASD find it difficult to place themselves in (the realm of thought of) others. It is difficult for them to envisage what other people think or feel. This causes insecurities in social interaction; predicting the way people will respond often doesn't pan out, and a person's intentions are often difficult to understand.

*A boy comes to the kitchen table for dinner. After a couple of bites, he says, 'This is disgusting.' His aunt, who's visiting them, tells him that she actually cooked this instead of his mother. The boy replies, 'Is that supposed to make it taste any better?'*

People without autism think in a type of circle: from themselves to the other and back again. They compare themselves to others and their relation to the world. Being able to compromise is part of that.

People with ASD often start out by thinking from their own perspective outward. This is why they will reach only one truth: their own. 'I am always right, and I don't deviate from that' is an expression that fits autism pretty well. People who have autism might be excellent observers, but at the same time they'll miss a lot of information.

Individuals with ASD who have a higher intelligence can be able to compensate for their autism by applying the Theory of Mind consciously. In that case, a conscious ToM doesn't come intuitively or automatically. Since it is taught, it works slower and is more difficult to apply in social situations.

## Executive Functioning

'Executive functions' are the higher controlling functions in the brain. These control functions play an important role in impulse control, planning and flexibility. People with ASD encounter problems here in self-organisation. These problems arise in the following areas, amongst others: targeted problem solution, planning step-by-step, impulse control, suppressing obvious but incorrect responses, adapting strategies, organised searching, and self-monitoring.

## The Absent Self

The absent self, originating from Uta Fruth, seems an overarching theory. This theory assumes a less present inner director in people with ASD. 'The big boss', the consciousness that regulates, oversees, and intervenes when things go wrong. You could compare it to a factory; everything works perfectly as it always does, but when the routine is gone or something happens unexpectedly, everything goes off track. Especially when the factory boss isn't available.

In his book Autism and Asperger Syndrome (The Facts), autism expert Simon Baron-Cohen discusses two new psychological theories about the background of autism: the theory of empathising versus systematising, and the magnocellular theory.

## Empathising versus Systematising

As there is an impairment and shortage in empathetic capacities in people with ASD, social and communicative problems arise. At the same time, this theory explains the stronger points of people with ASD – their ability to systematise.

Systematising is the urge to analyse or develop systems. These systems can come in many shapes or forms, but mostly it has to do with rules. In his study, Baron-Cohen also elaborates on the differences between the female brain (with a predisposition towards empathising) and the male brain (with a predisposition towards systematising). Individuals with ASD, he argues, possess an extremely 'male' brain; he connects this to the presence of testosterone in the developing male foetus.

Baron-Cohen's theory assumes that people with ASD are inclined towards technical details and results (systematising) and less on contact and co-operation (empathising).

**Magnocellular Theory**

The magnocellular theory aims to explain autism as due to a shortage in the visual system of the brain. In this theory, it is assumed – and partly proven – that there is a shortage in the magnocellular system, with which an individual perceives contrasts and movements. The parvocellular system, which accounts for depth and colour, does function properly. According to this theory, people with ASD would prefer avoiding moveable stimuli. What it does not account for, however, is how intrigued children with ASD can be by moving objects, such as the washing machine or marbles.

A second objection to this theory is that individuals with dyslexia also show magnocellular abnormalities, which is why it isn't clear if it can explain ASD as well. (I must add that I haven't been able to find this in the previous theories, either.)

As I discussed in a previous chapter ('Stimuli'), it is known that people with ASD don't just have trouble with visual stimuli; other sensory stimuli, such as sound and temperature, can also cause trouble.

Lastly, it has been established that people with ASD have noticed changes faster than neurotypicals. Studying the discrepancies in these studies is definitely a priority for the future.

All in all: there still is no 'one' theory. There is not one theory that is applicable to everyone with autism, but multiple might be applicable to one person. I wholeheartedly agree with Natasja's statement:

Natasja:
*'In studies about autism, the researchers often focus on how autistic people deviate from neurotypicals, and I think that's a shame. What they notice, for instance, is that autists have*

*difficulty with social cohesion and communication, which is incredibly important for neurotypicals. And then there are many theories made up around those findings, as if that is the 'core' of autism, as if autism is a social disorder. That isn't all too helpful if the core of autism lies somewhere completely different. In my opinion, it lies with the processing of information (that is, everything that needs to be processed: sounds, scents, language/communication, hunger/thirst, emotions, feelings, urges, nutrition, hormones, medication, etc).'*

# U NSUSPECTING

I notice that I can be quite unsuspecting and naïve at times. I've always believed that people don't lie, because I don't do it – that is, not consciously. Over time I've learnt that not everyone is to be trusted.

In the past, I used to be very open about what I had and what I had been through, but I've noticed that I am much more cautious about these things when I'm at work. Although I don't have any hard proof for it, I think it's been used against me once or twice. I've had the same thing in friendships. It occurred too often that I thought someone didn't mean it when they said something harsh, or that a friendship would improve with time. But the opposite appeared to be true. As a result, I remained in some relationships or friendships for too long, because I kept on thinking that it would all work out fine in the end.

Kimberley:
*'Yes, I'm incredibly unsuspecting. I find it impossible to believe that anyone would do something with bad intentions, because I would never do it myself. That also has to do with my lack of imagination. Luckily my nativity hasn't had any bad consequences yet.'*

Rob B:
*'I am terribly naïve. Usually I don't mind; in fact, I find it quite pleasant. In learning through experience I am consciously more realistic, and sometimes more sceptical. It once again boils down to knowing, thinking rationally. It's like everything else*

*that requires thought and watchfulness: every time it requires energy, no matter how well I believe these things to be in my system already.'*

Sandra:

*'Naïve people are much nicer! I'm pretty naïve myself. No, I don't believe everything, even if someone is able to tell it masterfully sadly. There simply are some people who clearly tell me their stories to attract my attention, whether this be consciously or subconsciously. I don't fall for every joke, either, so not everyone can lead me to believe anything. However, I will fall for traps more easily, and I am easier to manipulate than others. I know this, though, and I'm very aware of my vulnerability in this area.*

*Relationships and friendships have caused me some pain. That's the reason for my keeping distance of people, until I know if they're worthy of my trust.'*

Hans:

*'I have been very gullible in the past. I'm probably still naïve in some respects, but I have learnt learn by (bitter) experience, as I think people should. I'm just more distant towards others in many situations; I'll just have a chat, and that's it.'*

# VISITORS

Many people with ASD don't always like being with people. For me, I notice that it takes a lot of energy to have to talk all the time. Communicating with good friends isn't that difficult, but I think it's terrible to have to keep talking in a conversation with people I don't know. Also, I hardly ever care for what people tell me anyway.

Communicating in itself can be very exhausting for me, because I want to keep track of when it is my turn, when I am allowed to talk without interrupting someone else. And sometimes I simply don't understand what people are trying to tell me, because I trail off on some detail.

Birthday parties are one of the most ridiculous festivities ever invented. You're sitting in a circle, around a table with a bowl of peanuts everyone grabs for with their (dirty) hands, when the person next to you suddenly asks, 'So, what do you do for a living?' The next time when someone asks me this question – if it happens again – I decided to say, 'I'm a psychiatrist', or, 'I do pest control'. Oh, and the person you're there for, the one whose birthday it is, is, of course, inapproachable. Obviously, they'll be busy pouring drinks or refilling the snack bowl.

Yes, I also celebrate my birthday, but in an adapted way. Usually I'll say, 'It's self-service' or arrange for someone to do the refilling of drinks and snacks. I also make sure that the people I invite know one another, so questions about one's daily routine need not be asked.

Funnily enough, I'm someone who likes to be amongst people sometimes, but these are the people I choose myself. I work, for instance, with people with dementia. I love being around them; I think it's because they communicate differently. It's much more about the basic things, and I like that. I'll give people their coffees, help people with their food when they have trouble swallowing, and try to console them when they are anxious. I always say it's the best job I know. When you make someone happy by giving them a cup of coffee, their smile is priceless.

Anna:
*'I feel a bit like a failure. Half of my SST-group is going to a meeting place for people with ASD and I'm at home. I'm too passive and hardly do anything. At the same time, I'm incredibly jealous of others with autism who meet all throughout the country, when I'm not really able to do that. But, well, I don't really feel like going somewhere and experiencing such meetings negatively, because I can't seem to connect with them either.'*

Kimberley:
*'I really like making music – I play in an orchestra – and that's when I am pretty good around people. When I'm with friends, I think it's fun as well, but I do have to recharge for a while afterwards. When it comes to 'company' of people I don't know... I really dislike it. When we have unknown visitors at home I'll always go upstairs and hope they won't stay for too long.*

*I absolutely hate parties... having many people in a small space. Usually I only know a few of the people there, and I can't talk to people I don't know. I'll just stand there, getting more and more over-stimulated. I always try to leave no sooner than is 'acceptable', but I find it difficult to judge when exactly that is.'*

Anna:

*'I've been to the meeting-place for people with autism a couple of times. Some interesting people gather there. Autism basically radiates off them, if you will. To be honest, I almost feel almost 'normal' and as such stand out. It's difficult to get used to my diagnosis.'*

Hans:

*'I've hardly ever felt comfortable in company; though, I did realise over the last couple of years that I have a need for social interaction. I go to day time activities partly because of social contact. I seldom visit people, and have even less visitors, which I quite like. Sometimes I'll invite people over (to date, this is only family), but when they are in my house I (intuitively) want them to leave as soon as possible. I feel most lonely in company.'*

Sandra:

*'I definitely need company, but I often find that a lot of contacts I have don't really mean a lot to me. You either chat or you hear chitchat, about pets or anything other trivial you happen to share, and that's it. Those acquaintances are basically only functional. I don't really care for that type of company, and people tend to disappear from my radar, but I don't have any trouble with that. In fact, I find myself most confronted with my loneliness when I'm in company. It feels as if it works the other way as well; I can leave a gathering without leaving an empty spot. On occasion, it happens that I do like someone and than we keep contact in a way that's more than functional, which I really enjoy. I get attached to these people, so I'll talk and mail with them differently that I would with others, and I enjoy their company. I would love to be able to associate more with my*

*surroundings and feel more connected with people.*
*I also have the need to be alone. It doesn't even have to be*
*physically alone; when I'm with someone next to whom I can*
*just read in silence, that's fine as well. I quite like that, actually.*
*But after some time of being engaged with people, I have a*
*strong necessity to return to being introspective.'*

Khadijah:
*'I like company, but I also attach importance to my single life,*
*and the fact that I can retreat to have a good time in other ways*
*than social engagement. I have my contacts and I also tend to*
*go out for meetings. Via a different forum than this one, I found*
*a lot of friends, many of which I met in real life, and a friend*
*from Oujda (Morocco) stays over when she's headed this way.*
*That's at least two times per year. I also like getting to know*
*new people, but at a certain stage I prefer being alone again.*
*I'm alone, but definitely don't feel lonely.'*

Karen:
*'Sometimes I like being in company, but it's up to me to decide*
*when that is. The largest part of the day I prefer being alone.*
*It works pretty well for me, even though I live with six family*
*members. (Being alone = being introspective.)'*

Rob B.:
*'In social situations, like birthdays, I try to have something to do.*
*Once I did enjoy a big, convivial group, which was at a Hindu*
*wedding. The event lasted for a week, and we'd do everything*
*together: cooking, dancing, ceremonies with their priest, eating*
*together, and a lot more. For some reason I felt quite comfortable*
*doing all of that, regardless of the crowd, colours, loud music,*

*and the chatter and laughter of Hindu ladies I often didn't even understand. I thought it was wonderful, and I felt a pleasant connection with the group. Though being alone doesn't bother me at all, either.'*

# Withdrawing

From time to time, I love to withdraw in my home. I often do this when I'm tired or over- stimulated after doing something, such as grocery shopping. It happened more than once that I ended up insulting people in the supermarket, and I arrived home exhausted. It's difficult to explain to people without ASD how exactly this works. The presence of people alone already clouds my head, or products that are misplaced in the store... this list is endless. At home at last, I close my curtains, turn on my TV and collapse. Sometimes I go to sleep to refuel. I would love to be able to live during the night, when it's quiet and withdrawing is easier.

I also withdraw from friendships every once in a while, because I have too much to worry about, and I can't have anything else added to that. Some people may sense that something is wrong, as if I'm angry or something. Not everyone understands that I don't always feel like phoning or meeting.

When I'm somewhere and it's too much for me, I like to walk my dog. I prefer bringing her than leaving her at home, even if it's only to be able to handle situations like those. If I wouldn't allow myself to withdraw every once in a while, I might become depressed again and literally fall ill from stress.


Kimberley:
*'I withdraw when I'm over-stimulated. I have to be alone. When I was younger, my mum would want to go into town on Saturday afternoon, without announcing it. And when we got home, I would go up to my room immediately, which led to*

*misunderstandings ("You ruin the atmosphere immediately"). But I was over-stimulated, and I would actually ruin the atmosphere if I would stay downstairs and pretend to be 'fun' to be around. Because when I'm over-stimulated, I have an incredibly short fuse.'*

Sandra:

*'I tend to withdraw, but not always consciously. I can postpone it, but can't stop it. Being open to people all the time feels like I am an elastic band, being stretched out all the time, but wanting to go back to its original shape at one point. That is, I want to go back to being introspective. I zone out and tend to become a bit dreamy (I call this "spacing out"). Naturally when I'm tired or just not well, this happens more quickly than usual.*

*I also like doing something by myself – like reading or doing something on the computer – while others around me are doing other things. Growing up, everyone would do the same at the same time, like reading, alternated with activities to do together (conversation, games, walking, laughing). But I've also met people with whom it was impossible to go and read for myself. They grew angry with me or blamed me for shutting them out, even though there were many moments where we did connect. That's why I want people around me who don't demand my attention for twenty-four hours a day; they just have to accept that I'm not always available. Unless something serious is going on – if you just message me I'll be there for you, even if it's the middle of the night.'*

Hans:

*'I don't really need to withdraw at home, because I live on my own, and I don't really need it in the day centre, either. At events*

*that are more crowded, I do sometimes need it. And if I can't
take it I'll jump into stare-mode all the same. That's why I prefer
to be at the corner of a table when going to a restaurant with
a big group of people then I don't really have that problem. It
also happens that I become over-stimulated unconsciously, and
I realise I have to leave the situation, but the signal to get up and
leave doesn't come.*

*I don't want to avoid social activities too much. I do need it,
no matter how little. And the price, recovering for a week, is
worth it most of the time.'*

Natasja:

*'I completely withdrew from "ordinary" life, by living in a house
in a secluded area, and it suits me down to the ground. I try to
schedule my days in a way to not have to run into people too
much, apart from dancing every other week. Yesterday I went
online to look for housing agencies, just in case. But I get shivers
just thinking about living in the suburbs or something like that.'*

AQ:

*'I consciously withdraw when I want to keep my thoughts to
myself. That's got to do with the fact that I would want to say
something that might be too confronting to someone else. Since
I don't want to hurt this other person, I prefer not giving my
opinion at all.*

*I also withdraw when I want to think about something
without having to indulge in someone else's opinion first. I don't
know if it's necessary, but that's not how I use my moments of
silence. I use my silences where others use it for prayer, I am
silent because I am looking for a type of bridge between two
thoughts I'm balancing at the same time.'*

# Xeno

Xeno derives from the Greek xenos, which is often translated to 'stranger'. People with autism are often regarded as strangers; they behave differently, and that can scare people away. Even worse, it can lead to irritations, frustrations, sadness, and anger. A friend of mine once told me that, when he was little, his mother wanted to hug him, but he denied it because he didn't like physical contact. His mother often felt rejected and sad as a result.

In the 'Odd'-chapter, I already wrote about my time in high school, where children often didn't like me for my weird behaviour. Luckily, I did have a couple of friends there. I still find it difficult to connect with people. I am a chatterbox, but it remains hard to really bond with someone.

Something else that might make me a bit stranger than neurotypicals is that I take photographs of seemingly random things, stuff that people often don't really notice or take photos of. I'll give some examples: a close-up of a cigarette, rotting away in a bucket of dirty water; a urinating sheep; a row of pencils in a vase; two copulating flies; the bottom of a lantern post; etc.

Anna:
*'I think everybody else is different. It was quite difficult to be the only normal person in a world of strangers. I was bullied relentlessly in primary and secondary school. Later I learned how to fend for myself. In secondary school I was the nonconformist. That status did come with its benefits; I was the only one who was allowed to wear headgear in class. Some*

*teachers called me morbid; death and suicide played a big part in all of my papers. We used to be allowed to do that without being locked up back then. I only wore black clothing, because dark clothes best reflected my mood.'*

Kimberley:
*'For a very long time, I haven't felt different from other people, but I have no idea what other people thought of me. In secondary school, I started to get the feeling that I was different, and with that the feeling of being strange. I think that people actually thought of me as weird, especially classmates. I used to be very quiet, didn't say or ask anything. I did have conversations with friends, but never with anyone else in my grade. Sometimes someone tried, but I wasn't good at responding to them. After a while this happenstance contact became less and less, because people started to avoid me.*

*Some teachers also thought of me as weird. I've always been bad at French, for example. My mother had several conversations with my French teachers about it, and from fourth till sixth form they classified me as a "difficult" girl. I didn't like hearing my mother telling me that. I knew I was "different" (I didn't say anything during class), but I can't have been difficult. He should've formulated it differently. The problem wasn't that I was difficult myself, but that he found it difficult to work with me.*

*I'm happy I'm studying now. In the beginning I found the impersonality of university hard (I still do, by the way); you really are a number instead of a person. On the other hand, I like that nobody knows you, because nobody can think of you as weird.'*

Sandra:

*'I feel "different". In school we used to have the 'normal people' and the 'alternatives'. One day, an alternative boy came to me (new wave, very cool ;-)). He said he was jealous of me, because he was only pretending, whereas I really was different. I didn't have a lot to say to that at the time, but later I noticed I didn't like him saying that. At least he had a choice, and I didn't. Unfortunately I am very aware of my being strange to people, and that makes me feel like people don't like me. I know I'm weird. I've heard it a lot; people like me, but they don't know what to do with me. Sadly, the feeling is mutual at times. For that reason, it's very rare for an acquaintance to become a friend. Tough, because I'd like to know what it feels like to come somewhere, as an unfamiliar person, and to have the expectation of being known and accepted easily. Usually I feel like I speak a language that isn't understood, and although I can imitate the vernacular, it will never be my own.'*

Hans:

*'I think I've always felt different, but I never liked to be in the limelight or cultivate my being- different in any way. I can vaguely remember deciding that, if other children didn't need me, I didn't need them either. I must have been about seven years old. From that moment on I've been a loner, had some school "friends"... But that was mainly a situation of, "You have Lego, I have Lego. We're friends now." That's how easy it was back then.'*

# X-MAS STRESS

Christmas doesn't really mean a lot to me. Regardless of my Christian upbringing. It always felt more or less mandatory to visit our family on one of those days, because, hey, it's Christmas.

What I remember most from that time is that our dinner was more extravagant than during the rest of the year. Usually my mother would make roast with cranberries, and we'd have ice cream for dessert – something we'd always deduce from the small spoon next to our plates. My father read the Christmas story, and my sister, brother and I had usually rehearsed something to play on our musical instruments. My sister and I played the flute, and my brother the clarinet. The Christmas tree was always decorated entirely in silver, with lights that you could twist on and off. It would be the funniest thing if you'd turn it off by twisting the lamp that was the most difficult to find, so the person who had to turn on the tree wouldn't be able to do it.

On Boxing Day, I used to play Risk (one of those war-themed board games) with a friend who lived close by, even though war games aren't exactly in the spirit of Christmas. But, well, our "second day of Christmas" was a fake day anyway, because Jesus was born only once.

Natasja:
*'Although she's alone, my mother tends to make Christmas into a stone-grill or raclette evening, or she'll buy and decorate a small Christmas tree. My brother doesn't do anything, nor do I, and we all prefer to just sit at home. We don't have a lot of*

contact with our family members, and that sure makes the holiday season less stressful.'

Isa:

'We were never allowed to have arguments on Christmas, because it was Christmas. I thought that was nonsense... I don't have any good memories thinking about it, because the atmosphere was always tense, since we had to be nice to one another.'

Hans:

'Last Christmas I visited my family again for the first time in a long while. It was a lot of fun, I really enjoyed it, but it was exhausting as well. I used to cancel the Christmas parties I was invited to, and my mother would ask me if she was allowed to come visit me (it would be New Year's instead of Christmas), which was fine. All the 'quality time with family' and the bustle of the season... I often just don't feel like it, and I am happy that by now I'm able to cancel without many comments (this hasn't always been the case).'

Khadijah:

'I don't celebrate Christmas. I will go when one of my daughters invites me, though. Usually I'll end up in the kitchen, because my daughters are very chaotic ladies when it comes to cooking. And, since I want to eat in time, I'll have to take charge.

People generally know that I would rather not join in with festivities, and I prefer taking advantage of those days to get some rest. I'm happy that the supermarkets are open on these days, so even if you don't celebrate Christmas you'll still be able to use your days efficiently.'

# Y IN AND Y AN

The term yin-yang derives from Chinese, and covers certain oppositions that can't exist without one another. This principle is absorbed in all aspects of life. They aren't just oppositions, though, but also complementary values. Light can't exist without darkness, and love can't exist without hatred. It's nice when a balance can be found between these two.

Some examples of yin-yang principles are:

| Yin | Yang |
| --- | --- |
| Below | Above |
| Cold | Hot |
| Water | Fire |
| Female | Male |
| Moon | Sun |
| Black | White |
| Dark | Light |
| Passive | Active |
| Hatred | Love |
| Defence | Attack |
| Serenity | Action |
| Death | Life |

As Westerner, the Chinese way of thinking is difficult to really understand. Westerners tend to think in boxes. For example, we'd say 'the table is square and not round'. In traditional Chinese thought, however, the table can be both square and a little round.

The most important thing to take from this chapter is that the balance between two things is imperative.

In some ways, my life is quite balanced. When it comes to work, I'm good at setting boundaries, so it remains enjoyable and won't pull me under. In terms of love life, however, I'm really missing something. I'm not that good at relationships, and that makes me sad sometimes. I miss a buddy, someone who can put an arm around me at times; someone with whom I can undertake things; someone with whom I can share mutual interests. I miss someone who likes and loves me for who I am, and who wants to be with me. I think I could become more balanced if I had someone like that, given that it is a healthy relationship, of course.

When it comes to assistance and coaching, I can say my life is quite balanced. I have proper care at home by means of my PIP, both with individual coaching as well as housekeeping.

I've also found a good balance regarding serenity and action. I take part in many activities, but I also make sure that I have enough moments to rest beside that. Part of that is because, even in moments of rest, I'll already think about that what needs to happen when I'm done resting.

Hans:
*My zodiac sign is Libra, and I often blame the sign – a scale – for being imbalanced. That's how I've felt quite often, as well. However, since I know more about autism and have come into contact with other people with ASD, I've realised that I am actually relatively balanced. One day I couldn't go on holiday, because I spent nearly all of my money on boxes of Miles Davis (I really obsessed over that). Not quite balanced, but I don't regret that decision.*

*I put my social interaction – meetings in particular – on the back burner for a while. It can hardly be combined with day centre and a studying-from-home programme I'm picking up again.*

*There are some events that I have so much fun attending that I almost forget what I'm like after having been to someplace busy. Well, that's when I notice why I've been declared unfit for work.'*

# Zest

By 'zest' I mean the enthusiasm for having a hobby or activity in which you can really lose yourself. Many people with ASD find relaxation in engaging in their zests (for ease, I'll also refer to them as 'obsessions', although there is a difference!). Sometimes people have one of these activities, something they spend a lot of time in doing and can be really good at; others have several. What's more, their object of enthusiasm can change over the years. My personal biggest obsession is my dog, Daisy. I can also really lose myself in photography.

An obsession I used to have is chess; when I was a child I used to replay matches by the grandmasters until I found the best opening move for myself. An older obsession – one that came back during the Winter Olympics – is ice skating, but especially watching it on TV. I used to keep track of the lap records with a pen in the newspaper; I couldn't bear missing a race! And I used to share my enthusiasm with others, not knowing that it was a very boring and annoying monologue for my uninterested classmates, who would rather do something else. Now I'm still glued to the tube for every ice-skating race – without pen and paper, but with my phone in hand to take pictures and post them on Facebook when yet another Dutch contestant has won gold.

As for my current interest, my dog Daisy... I can write about her for hours. She's my biggest friend and I don't know what I'd do without her. My last dog, Clint, was my first -zest- dog, and Daisy is a great second one. It's an art to not talk too much about her to others, because – being a true autist – I tend to lose track of when I'm too much involved in my own world, talking too much about my obsession. The best thing for me to do is just to talk to other dog owners about Daisy, because the majority shows obsessive behaviour when it comes to their pet, even if they don't have ASD.

A couple of years ago, I had a zest when it came to medication. I might as well have been a medical encyclopaedia. I knew basically all side effects and dosages of anti-depressants. At present, it has moved more towards watching documentaries about medical cases: scary diseases, unknown conditions – they're all very interesting to me. I'm also interested in crime and murder shows on channels like TLC; I'm fascinated by people's motives to commit certain crimes.

Of course, there are many other obsessions as well. A fellow autist, for example, once built a lightning machine. For the enthusiasts: a Testla Coil, with which he was able to produce lightning bolts of three metres. They release around 800,000 Volt! There are only a couple of people in the world that build devices like these. They aren't toys, though, and require a lot of knowledge and caution. I have no idea how they work, but I think it's truly beautiful to look at.

These 'zests' can also tend towards compulsive and obsessive behaviour. I try to watch out for that, because it can make me restless. When I think, 'I have to see all the pictures on my computer, even if that means pulling an all-nighter', it becomes obsessive. Needless to say, that isn't too good for me. It remains difficult to snap out of it in time.

Here are a couple of these zests I know others to have:
- Looking at skeletons of dead animals
- Insects
- Mythology
- Model trains
- Miles Davis
- Progressive rock
- Veganism
- Cooking
- Morocco
- Writing

Hans:
*'I've had many different zests in the past, and every single time it felt as if that object of obsession was the best thing ever! And then I'd lose my interest in a couple of years or months... Ugh. I haven't had a good, persistent one in some years, and in all honesty I kind of miss it.'*

Khadijah:
*'Sometimes I join in with my son's zests, just because it's nice to feel his enthusiasm for them.'*

Anna:
*'Today in my course on psycho-education we got to tell about our special interest. There was a chef in our group, whose passion was to bake cakes, and he made an amazing one. Yum! Not too great for one's diet, but incredibly delicious.*
*I no longer really have a special obsessive interest. I brought a couple of old books: a Bible from the late-eighteenth century*

*and a book from the nineteenth century. I brought them to tell a bit about my extinct obsession with theology. The Bible was an edition of the first direct translation of the Bible into Dutch, and one of the course instructors called the language Old Dutch. I loved the ignorance; it is – obviously – written in Early Modern Dutch. Old Dutch is characterised very differently by full vowels near the closing consonants. But that aside.*

*Speaking of hobby's... The lack of an obsessive interest causes kind of a hole in my day. I get incredibly bored when I've finished all my housekeeping chores.*

*Sometimes I'll fill the time on shady websites, reading nonsense about the Illuminati (the term for several historical 'secret' communities), freemasons, and the New World Order. But this misinformation doesn't exactly cheer me up. Perhaps I should look for books on poisonous snakes, because that's also a small interest of mine. The black mamba is a truly fascinating creature. Sadly, though, there isn't a lot written about this snake, because it's too dangerous to study.'*

# A FINAL NOTE

Writing this book was an incredible journey, both for me and for the people on our forum, who helped me create this ABC about ASD. Without them, this book would never have been as complete as it is now. On the forum, we've also chatted about these topic a bit further than what I've put in this book. I feel like I've gotten to know my ASD-buddies even better. I definitely found it very enjoyable and educational. I'd also like to take this moment to thank them all; many thanks!

Thanks to Sandra, Natasja, Rob B., Marc, Hans, Kimberley, AQ, Rob, Karen (Willeke), Khadijah, and Anne!

I also would like to thank Angélique van Ewijk, who did the first corrections on the manuscript, and Aviva Dassen for her translation of the book from Dutch into English.
Lastly, I'd also like to thank my brother for taking the picture on the back cover.

Sandra:
*'I've found helping with your book an incredibly educational experience. It didn't just make me consider how I bring across the way I view things, but also made me aware of the way other people with ASD experience their worlds. Of course, it is pretty nerve-wrecking to be quoted in a book that might be read by quite some people. I've put quite some energy in it, but I think it's important to put energy into things that create more understanding for autism and give it a human face.'*

Hans:

*'Several topics arose during the making of this book, many of which I generally don't think about. I always take my autism more or less as a given fact, but it can be enlightening to think about how things work for me in contrast to others. My experiences don't have to be the same as anyone else's.'*

Khadijah:

*'For me, it was a motivation to think about and look at myself, ranging from things that were obvious to me to self-analysis and acceptance. Thank you for taking the effort to write this book. I hope it'll serve as an inspiration for many, for people who seek recognition and answers on the daily issues that colour our lives the way they do.'*

Printed in Great Britain
by Amazon

42971981R00075